Tablet PCs
in K–12 Education

Edited by

Mike van Mantgem

Contributions by

Dave Berque, Edward J. Evans, Tracy Hammond,
Kenrick Mock, Mark Payton, and David S. Sweeney

International Society for Technology in Education
EUGENE, OREGON • WASHINGTON, DC

Tablet PCs in K–12 Education

EDITED BY MIKE VAN MANTGEM

Director of Book Publishing: *Courtney Burkholder*
Director of Business Development for Educational Leadership: *Mark P. Andrews*
Acquisitions Editor: *Jeff V. Bolkan*
Production Editor: *Lynda Gansel*
Production Coordinator: *Maddelyn High*
Graphic Designer and Cover Design: *Signe Landin*
Book Sales and Marketing Manager: *Max Keele*
Copyeditor: *Tim A. Taylor*
Indexer: *Ken Hassman, Hassman Indexing Services*
Book Design and Production: *Kim McGovern*

Library of Congress Cataloging-in-Publication Data

Tablet PCs in K-12 education / edited by Mike van Mantgem; contributions by
   Dave Berque ... [et al.]. — 1st ed.
     p. cm. — (National educational technology standards for students
   curriculum series)
   Includes bibliographical references and index.
   ISBN 978-1-56484-241-1 (pbk.)
   1. Computer-assisted instruction. 2. Pen-based computers.   I. Van
Mantgem, Mike. II. Berque, Dave A., 1963- III. International Society for
Technology in Education. IV. Title: Tablet personal computers in K-12 education.
   LB1028.5.T318 2008
   371.33′4416—dc22

                                                                    2008018118

First Edition
ISBN: 978-1-56484-241-1

Printed in the United States of America

International Society for Technology in Education (ISTE)
Washington, DC, Office:
     1710 Rhode Island Ave. NW, Suite 900, Washington, DC 20036-3132
Eugene, Oregon, Office:
     175 West Broadway, Suite 300, Eugene, OR 97401-3003
Order Desk: 1.800.336.5191
Order Fax: 1.541.302.3778
Customer Service: orders@iste.org
Book Publishing: books@iste.org
Rights and Permissions: permissions@iste.org
Web: www.iste.org

About ISTE

The International Society for Technology in Education (ISTE) is the trusted source for professional development, knowledge generation, advocacy, and leadership for innovation. A nonprofit membership association, ISTE provides leadership and service to improve teaching, learning, and school leadership by advancing the effective use of technology in PK–12 and teacher education.

Home of the National Educational Technology Standards (NETS), the Center for Applied Research in Educational Technology (CARET), and the National Educational Computing Conference (NECC), ISTE represents more than 85,000 professionals worldwide. We support our members with information, networking opportunities, and guidance as they face the challenge of transforming education. To find out more about these and other ISTE initiatives, visit our Web site at **www.iste.org.**

As part of our mission, ISTE Book Publishing works with experienced educators to develop and produce practical resources for classroom teachers, teacher educators, and technology leaders. Every manuscript we select for publication is carefully peer-reviewed and professionally edited. We look for content that emphasizes the effective use of technology where it can make a difference—increasing the productivity of teachers and administrators; helping students with unique learning styles, abilities, or backgrounds; collecting and using data for decision making at the school and district levels; and creating dynamic, project-based learning environments that engage 21st-century learners. We value your feedback on this book and other ISTE products. E-mail us at **books@iste.org.**

About the Contributors

Mike van Mantgem has been writing and editing books about technology use since 1994. He earned his English/Language Arts teaching certification from the University of Iowa.

Dave Berque is a professor of computer science at DePauw University in Greencastle, Indiana.

Edward J. Evans is the interim executive director of IT for Teaching and Learning Technologies at Purdue University in Indiana.

Tracy Hammond is an assistant professor in the Department of Computer Science at Texas A&M University.

Kenrick Mock is an associate professor in the Department of Mathematical Sciences at the University of Alaska, Anchorage.

Mark Payton is the director of information resources and technology at Vermont Academy.

David S. Sweeney is the director for information technology in the Division of Student Affairs at Texas A&M University.

Acknowledgements

The International Society for Technology in Education (ISTE) would like to thank many organizations and individuals for their generous support in the publication of *Tablet PCs in K–12 Education*.

The book's publication was made possible in part by Hewlett-Packard (HP), and many of HP's staff served as manuscript reviewers. ISTE is greatly appreciative of HP's support of our mission to improve teaching and learning by advancing the effective use of technology in education. ISTE also thanks David S. Sweeney of Texas A&M University, who originally organized the contributing authors. These authors were all very professional and easy to work with, and they provided the knowledge and expertise required to create this valuable educator resource. PotomacPlanet also played a large role by supporting the book's vision, supplying case studies and lesson plans, and assisting in editorial components. Finally, the book's editor, Mike van Mantgem, provided the technical skills necessary to create an easy-to-navigate handbook for tablet PC users and educators.

For their efforts, everyone mentioned has ISTE's sincerest appreciation.

MARK P. ANDREWS, M.ED.
ISTE's Director of Business Development for Educational Leadership
Project Director of *Tablet PCs in K–12 Education*

This book's publication was made possible in part by the generous support of Hewlett-Packard.

Global citizenship is one of HP's longstanding corporate objectives, and social investment is one of the many ways HP demonstrates its commitment to being a good corporate citizen. Our education investments are geared toward transforming teaching and increasing student success, particularly in math, science, and engineering. The HP Technology for Teaching Program has awarded nearly $50 million in cash and equipment to 840 educational institutions in 36 countries around the world.

Contents

Introduction

DAVID S. SWEENEY
Director for Information Technology
Division of Student Affairs
Texas A&M University

This book is a practical guide for educators to use tablet PCs to instruct, communicate, and collaborate in the classroom. Throughout, you'll find examples and case studies taken from real teachers in real classrooms. Theory and research are included at the end of most chapters, for those of you who may be interested in these topics. However, the primary focus of this book is on the practical use of tablet PCs in the classroom.

We have assembled a team of knowledgeable contributors, many of whom are associated with the Workshop on the Impact of Pen-Based Technology on Education (WIPTE) and are, quite frankly, leading the dialog on the use of tablet PCs in education.

In Part I, you will be introduced to the tablet PC as a communication and computing platform. These chapters will describe some of the more common software applications used with tablets. Here, you will also find real-world examples of tablet PC use, key resources, and a glossary of this book's computing terms.

Part II moves from information about tablet PC computing and into educational applications. In these chapters you will see just how the tablet PC can improve personal productivity for both you and your students; how to use the tablet PC in single-user (that is, non-collaborative) settings; just how the tablet PC can revolutionize collaborative, 1-to-1 learning environments; and finally, how to implement tablet PCs in your organization. All told, Part II should prove invaluable for educators, administrators, and technical support personnel as they consider how to deploy tablet PCs in a classroom, across a school, or throughout a district.

Part III utilizes the knowledge presented in the previous two sections by offering real-world lesson plans optimized for the tablet PC.

I've been humbled to work with our contributing team during the course of writing this book. I would like to personally thank Kenrick Mock, Tracy Hammond, Mark Payton, Dave Berque, and Ed Evans for their contributions. Thanks also to Craig Colgan for his consultations. Mark Andrews at the International Society for Technology in Education (ISTE) was especially helpful. Our editor, Mike van Mantgem, who kept us on track, deserves many kudos. Having cold-called many of these fine professionals to collaborate on this book, I'm deeply gratified by their willingness to contribute, and I hope to work with them again.

Thank you.

How to Use this Book

The goal of this book is simple: To provide educators with a hands-on look at the tablet PC and to show them how to best utilize this technology in the classroom. Neither educators nor their students need to be technophiles to benefit from the information this book offers. To get the most out of this book:

- **Part I.** Consult the "Glossary of Terms" and the other information in chapter 1 to get acquainted with some tablet PC basics. If you are new to tablet PCs, you won't believe what you'll find.

- **Part II.** Discover the ways in which the tablet PC can increase your own personal productivity and improve the classroom experience for you and your students. The ideas in this section come from the world's leading tablet PC thinkers in education.

- **Part III.** Explore the lesson plans. Straightforward and easy to read, these content- and grade-specific lessons are designed for you to use and modify in your own classrooms. (See Lesson Plans: At a Glance on page 3.)

- Peruse the examples found in "Tablet PCs in the Real World" boxes throughout the book. You'll find the stories of other educators who have found a place for tablet PC technology in their own classrooms. Where they have gone, you can go, too. (See Tablet PCs in the Real World: At a Glance on page 4.)

Lesson Plans: At a Glance

Special Education

- Adding and Subtracting Fractions (*Mathematics; features extensions for K–2 and 3–6*)

  Students map out the steps necessary for adding and subtracting fractions with uncommon denominators and then simplify the answer. Tablet PCs or PDAs are used to map out the solution with concept-mapping software. Lesson adaptations show how to use this strategy to teach other math concepts.

Grades K–2

- Animals of North America (*Science, Mathematics*)

  Becoming virtual zoologists, students research, collect, and report data on the various animals of Canada, Mexico, and the United States. Students work independently or in groups to create a multimedia PowerPoint presentation on a North American animal.

- Brrr, It's Alive (*English Language Arts*)

  Students write a riddle that gives clues about a cold-weather animal. Other students try to guess the animal's identity. The information gathered to create the riddle forms the foundation for writing a report about cold-weather animals.

Grades 3–5

- Exploring Wetlands (*Science*)

  Students see videos of marsh and wetland areas and locate these areas on Google Earth. Then students research a wetland animal and create a riddle about the animal in PowerPoint. These riddles are posted to the school's wetlands Web site for other students to read.

- Fairytales Compare and Contrast (*English Language Arts*)

  In a teacher-led demonstration, students differentiate story aspects of two versions of *Hansel and Gretel*, told from two different points of view. Independently, students read similar stories and compare and contrast fairytale characteristics using concept-mapping software.

Grades 6–8

- The Scientific Method (*Science*)

  After studying the scientific method, students go through the process of developing a hypothesis, performing an experiment, showing findings, and analyzing results.

- Birthstone Project (*English Language Arts, Science*)

  This lesson is an interdisciplinary project for an English/language arts teacher, an earth science teacher, and a technology teacher. Students learn about their birthstones—and minerals in general—through online research, writing, and development of an electronic presentation.

Grades 9–12

- Habitat Investigation (*Science*)

  Using a custom-created Web site and supporting materials, students learn about a natural habitat in their community, including the geology, topography, plants, animals, and human activities.

- Lining Up Data (*Mathematics*)

  Students make predictions based on real-world data. Students use the tablet PC to plot data and draw lines that fit the data they have graphed. They then use these lines to make predictions that extrapolate or interpolate the data. Students conduct additional research to find appropriate data sets, develop questions, and answer questions developed by other students.

Tablet PCs in the Real World: At a Glance

This book contains many illustrations and real-world examples of tablet PCs and their use in the classroom. Below is a quick index of where you'll find these powerful stories.

Personal Computing Made Personal. It's not so much a matter of what a tablet PC can *do*, but what a tablet PC *is*. Page 37.

Taking Notes: A Small Demonstration. A single demonstration was all it took for one educator to implement a tablet PC pilot program. Page 63.

Vermont Academy: The Personal Productivity of Students. Students at a small, rural independent boarding and day school use tablet PCs to increase their productivity. Page 81.

Colorado School for the Deaf and the Blind: Using Technology to Improve Student Learning and Build a Professional Learning Community. Educators use digital photography and tablet PCs to both aid in student learning and to better understand the learning process of their students. Page 83.

Ferryway School: Using 21st-Century Technology to Study the Technological Needs of Colonists in the New World. Students use modern technology to learn about the uses of technology at a colonial ironworks. Page 91.

St. Martin's Episcopal School: Teaching 11th- and 12th-Grade Pre-Calculus, Calculus, and Trigonometry. A Louisiana high school math instructor creates innovative video recordings of lectures. Page 99.

Goldenview Middle School: Teaching Eighth-grade Algebra and Pre-Algebra. An Alaska math instructor uses a tablet PC to post lecture notes and assignments online. Page 102.

DyKnow Vision in Action. An illustration of how a classroom teacher promotes in-class collaboration while teaching a basic math problem. Page 125.

Bishop Hartley High School: Partnering with Higher Education to Assess a 1-to-1 Tablet Deployment. One private school and a neighboring state university work together to bring tablet PCs into the classroom. Page 129.

Auburn City Schools: A Model Faculty Development Program in the Context of a 1-to-1 Tablet Deployment. A thoughtful approach to deploying a 1-to-1 tablet PC program generates a solid buy-in from teachers and enhances student engagement. Page 131.

Memorial Middle School: Quality Counts—Partnership with HP. Classroom teachers describe the extent that quality matters when a school chooses its technology partner. Page 141.

The tablet PC is unlike any other computing device that has come before
it. A tablet PC combines the computing power and versatility of a traditional notebook computer with the portability, inking ability, and ease of
use offered by a pad of paper. It is small enough to carry anywhere, yet
large enough to replace a desktop computer, filing cabinet, and a small
library, essentially allowing a user to take the classroom on the road.

But what exactly *is* a tablet PC? What *exactly* does it allow users to do?
Moreover, how does this technology fit into an educational setting?

Answers to these questions, and more, are here.

1

From
Convertibles to Slates

MORE THAN A NOTEBOOK

KENRICK MOCK
Associate Professor, Department of Mathematical Sciences
University of Alaska, Anchorage

TRACY HAMMOND
Assistant Professor, Department of Computer Science
Texas A&M University

With contributions from:
MIKE VAN MANTGEM
Editor, ISTE

What Is a Tablet PC?

In general terms, a tablet PC is a notebook computer with a display screen on which users can "write." The computer's operating system allows digital "ink" to be written or drawn on the computer screen by using a special pen. This process is called "digital inking," and hand-drawn items can be saved like any other computer document. Handwritten text can also be saved "as written," or it can be translated into typed text.

FIGURE 1.1. | The tablet PC

Microsoft Tablet PC

The term "tablet PC" was coined by Microsoft when it released its Windows XP Tablet PC operating system. Consequently, an official Microsoft Tablet PC is essentially a notebook computer with a touch- or pen-enabled screen (digitizer) running Windows XP Tablet PC Edition or Windows Vista.

Since digital inking is added to the normal functionality of a personal computer, applications that run on a personal computer (such as Word or PowerPoint) also run on a tablet PC.

At the time of this writing, Microsoft Windows devices dominate the market for tablet PCs. The technology has also matured since its introduction, as many tablet PC models are now entering their fourth or fifth generation. According to TabletPCReview. com, there are currently more than 20 manufacturers of tablet PCs encompassing more than 50 different models (TabletPCReview, 2007).

From Punch Cards to Digital Ink
A Brief History of the Tablet PC

In 1968 the UNIVAC 9200 computer ran on punch cards, had a memory of 16,386 bytes, and cost $1,000 per month to rent. Despite the prevalence of these room-sized mainframes, in 1968 computer scientist Alan Kay envisioned a computer that could be used effortlessly by untrained users. He proposed a device called the Dynabook, which was lightweight, could communicate wirelessly, and could electronically store notes written with a pen. His vision was partially fulfilled by many devices built in the 1980s and '90s, including the Apple Newton and the Personal Digital Assistant (Meyer, 1995). Kay's vision was fully realized with the introduction of the tablet PC in 2002.

Why Use a Tablet PC in the Classroom?

If using notebook computers in a classroom is a good practice, then employing tablet PCs represents a revolution.

Despite the many advantages of computer-aided instruction, so-called normal notebook computers are restricted by their keyboard/mouse inputs. A keyboard has its limits, and a mouse is very difficult to use for sketching—it does not have the natural feel of a pen, nor does it provide a pen's accuracy.

Because students and teachers alike can write, draw, and sketch with freedom directly into a tablet PC, they can:

- Tap directly into their creative brainstorming thought-processes;

- Simulate, correct, and perform sophisticated editing commands with the ease of a pen-stroke; and

- Easily share their creations with others in real time, using a variety of applications (described at the end of this chapter).

Tablet PCs place these technologies into the hands of students, creating a more effective active learning environment. If the traditional computer allows for a functional understanding of instructional material to students, then it follows that the natural feel of a pen-input interface can actually encourage creativity. The tablet PC thus allows students to work seamlessly between two different types of pedagogical visualizations (Hammond, 2007a).

Glossary of Terms

What follows are essential tablet PC computing terms. Familiarity with these terms will greatly enhance your ability to think about, talk about, and teach about tablet PCs.

Tablet-Specific Terms

Notebook Computer. Also known as a laptop computer, a notebook computer is a computer designed primarily for portability.

Tablet PC. A notebook computer that allows users to input information on a digitizer with a pen, or stylus.

Display. In this context, a screen that shows a computer's output information.

Digitizer. The technology located in a tablet PC's display (screen) that allows it to determine the location of a device writing on the display. A passive digitizer uses touch (a touch-screen). An active digitizer detects electromagnetic signals from a special pen. A hybrid digitizer combines the passive digitizer's convenience of touch with the active digitizer's superior handwriting-recognition capabilities.

Pen. Resembling a traditional ink pen, a Pen is a specialized input device that allows users to write directly on the screen (digitizer) of a tablet PC.

Stylus. A stylus is a type of pen that typically does not "ink" a tablet PC's screen. Rather, a stylus is used in place of a finger to interact with a touch-screen.

Digital Ink; Ink. Data put directly onto the tablet PC's digitizer. The process of inputting data in this manner is called "digital inking."

Pen Flicks. Gestures that users make with their tablet PC pens to perform quick navigation tasks (drag up, drag down, move back, etc.) and utilize shortcuts (copy, paste, undo, etc.). Using macros, a single pen flick can be made to perform a customized sequence of computing functions.

> ## PUTTING IT TOGETHER
>
> Since a Tablet PC is essentially a special type of notebook computer, it shares the same hardware features as a typical notebook computer with the exception of the digitizer that enables pen input.

Macros. A computing rule or pattern that specifies how a certain input sequence should be mapped to an output sequence.

TIP. Short for Tablet Input Panel. A Windows control that translates the user's ink strokes into typed text.

Lasso. A drawing tool that allows users to draw a freehand perimeter around a section of the screen; then, to select and manipulate that portion.

Vectoring. An occurrence of when a user's palm touches the screen of a tablet PC and triggers an unintended "click."

Hardware Terms

Form Factor. This term refers to the overall design of something. In the case of a tablet PC, the two most common form factors are the slate and the convertible.

Slate. The slate form of a tablet PC resembles a large PDA, or writing "slate." This form of a tablet PC does not have an attached keyboard.

Convertible. The convertible form of a tablet PC resembles a traditional notebook computer, except that its screen can twist and rotate such that the display is facing out when it's folded down over the keyboard.

Multi-Touch PC. A computer that allows multiple users to simultaneously manipulate objects on the screen by touch.

Ultra Mobile PC (UMPC). An Ultra Mobile PC, or UMPC, is a small-form tablet PC that is designed to fit into pockets or small bags.

Personal Digital Assistant (PDA). A PDA is a hand-held device that is used to organize personal data. PDAs typically include some computer functionality and can have multimedia capabilities. As of this writing, Apple's iPhone is the latest showcase of PDA technology.

USB-Connected Pen Tablets. Light and portable tablets that allow pen-to-computer input, but do not provide display capabilities.

Interactive Whiteboard. A touch-sensitive screen technology that allows users to manipulate data directly on a digital display. In a classroom setting, an inter-active whiteboard can take the form of a touch-sensitive large screen display that connects to a computer and digital projector. Users can control computer applica-tions directly from the projected display, write notes in digital ink, and save their work.

Configuration. This term describes the summation of the devices associated with (and/or connected to) a given PC. Typically, these items include the computer (meaning, the internal hardware that comprises the computer), monitor, keyboard, printer, and so on.

CPU. Central Processing Unit. The brain of a personal computer.

RAM. Random Access Memory. This memory type allows computers to load and run programs or otherwise use data on a temporary basis. As a general rule, the more RAM a computer has, the more quickly it can process information.

x86-Compatible. This term refers to the compatibility among types and brands of computer microprocessors with the family of Intel microprocessors (e.g., Intel 486, Pentium, Intel 8086, etc.).

PUTTING IT TOGETHER

A common convertible tablet PC configuration today might include 1 GB of RAM, a 100-GB hard disk, a DVD/CD drive, assorted ports, and an x86-compatible CPU running Windows Vista.

Bit. The fundamental unit of computing information. A bit has only one of two values, either the binary digit 0 or 1.

Byte. A sequence of 8 bits, combined into a single unit of information.

Gigabyte; GB. 1 billion bytes. Used as a measure of data storage capacity or computer memory capacity.

Hard Disk. A rigid magnetic disk used for storing computer data. Also called a hard drive.

DVD/CD Drive. A device that reads (and writes to) both high-density compact discs (DVDs) and compact discs (CDs). When this device is built into a computer, it is often called an integrated optical drive.

Port. A distinct connection area on a computer that allows other devices to attach to, and communicate with, that computer. A USB (universal serial bus) is a type of port.

Operating System. Often referred to as an "O-S," this is the software that runs a computer. Popular PC operating systems include Windows (XP, Vista, etc.), Linux, and Mac OS (8, X, etc.).

Communications Terms

802.11. A set of standards for wireless local area network (WLAN) computer communication. As of this writing, 802.11n is the latest standard on the market.

Bluetooth. A short-range radio frequency standard that allows wireless communication among devices such as computers, cell phones, printers, digital cameras, and the like.

Cellular Networks. An interconnected system of mobile telephone transmitters. Each transmitter covers a distinct geographical area, or cell.

Client. A piece of software that resides on a user's computer (a client). This software accesses services from another piece of software on another computer (a server).

EV-DO. Evolution-Data Optimized. A telecommunications standard for transmitting data through radio signals.

IM. Short for Instant Messaging, a real-time communication software that allows two or more users to exchange typed text. The text is conveyed via computers connected over a network.

Internet. Small computer networks that link together to form a larger computer network. The Internet is the largest network.

LAN. Local Area Network. A communications network that covers a small area (e.g., a school building, a coffee shop, or an individual home).

Network. An interconnected system of computing devices. These devices transmit and receive data to and from each other.

Skype. An Internet telecommunications software, Skype allows users to make telephone calls from their computer to other computers, landlines, and cell phones.

PUTTING IT TOGETHER

With an emphasis on mobility, virtually all tablet PCs include support for wireless networking. More recent devices include support for wireless WAN over cellular networks, making it possible to access the Internet in any location where there is already cell phone coverage.

WAN. Wide Area Network. A communications network that covers a large geographic area.

WiMAX. Worldwide Interoperability for Microwave Access. A technology designed to provide wireless data transmission across long distances.

Wireless Network. A computer network where devices transmit and receive data without any physical connection between sender or receiver.

The Tablet PC: A Machine for Every Occasion

It is no accident that tablet PCs are not created equal. The dynamic nature of the technology behind these machines allows for a variety of uses that, in turn, meet an even wider variety of needs. The more you know about tablet PCs, the more informed you will be when thinking about and using tablet PCs in a classroom setting.

Passive Digitizers

To use a passive digitizer, one simply touches a PC's screen with a finger or stylus. This is the equivalent of a mouse click at the pressed location. An advantage of the passive digitizer is the ability to use one's finger or any stylus to interact with the device. A special pen is not required.

This form of interaction is particularly useful for screen navigation—it is more convenient and often feels more natural to "click" a button or scroll down by simply touching the screen or moving your finger, versus getting out a stylus and tapping the screen.

However, the convenience of a passive digitizer has several drawbacks:

- Writing on a passive digitizer can result in an effect called *vectoring*, which occurs when a touch on the screen triggers an unintended "click."

- The computer has no way to tell where the pen is located unless the pen touches the screen. When a pen is used for navigation, the result is a mouse cursor that jumps from touch-point to touch-point. This effect can make a presentation difficult to follow.

- Since a "click" is the only input (and is mapped to a tap), secondary functions such as right-clicking are more difficult to perform. Microsoft's operating system, for example, requires a user to tap-and-hold the stylus for right-click options.

- The resolution and accuracy of a passive digitizer is usually lower than that of an active digitizer. As a result, handwriting with a passive digitizer may appear "blocky" and "erratic" instead of smooth and free-flowing.

Active Digitizers

Most tablet PCs incorporate an active digitizer. This technology requires a special stylus to write on the display. The digitizer emits an electromagnetic signal from the display that is reflected by the stylus. The reflection is then used to determine the precise location of the stylus. This technology eliminates the vectoring problem, since touch is not used at all to determine the pen's location. In addition, the distance of the pen from the display can be tracked. This precise tracking allows for a "hover" mode in which the pen controls the cursor, but a click does not occur unless the pen makes contact with the display.

Digitizers in the Real World

The Wacom digitizer is the most common form of an active digitizer. If you have ever used a digital pen and pad to sign your name when making a credit card purchase, you are already familiar with how this technology works in the real world.

Using an active digitizer and a pen is similar to using a traditional mouse. The pen tip is easy to track while writing. Likewise, when giving a presentation, an audience can follow the pointer with ease.

Other advantages of an active over a passive digitizer include more nuanced pressure sensitivity (e.g., pushing the pen harder results in a thicker or darker line), superior precision, smoother ink, side buttons for more right-clicking options, and—using the top of the pen—a digital eraser.

The main disadvantage of the active digitizer is its reliance on a special pen. If the pen is lost, then the tablet's functionality becomes inaccessible. Additionally, active digitizers tend to be inaccurate near the borders of the display. Periodic calibration is also necessary to accurately track the pen's location.

Hybrid Digitizers

The hybrid digitizer combines the passive digitizer's convenience of touch with the active digitizer's superior handwriting capabilities—an all-in-one device. A button or switch on the computer enables the user to select which digitizer is preferred. Alternately, the computer has the option to sense if the active digitizer's pen is near the surface of the display, in which case the active digitizer is enabled and the passive digitizer is disabled. When the pen is not detected near the surface, the passive digitizer is enabled and the active digitizer is disabled.

Forms of Tablet PCs

The type of digitizer is an important consideration for tablet PC use in the classroom. An equally important consideration is the form of the computer itself. The two most common forms of tablet PCs are slate and convertible. The different design styles of tablet PCs are often referred to as form factors.

Slate

The slate tablet PC resembles a large PDA or writing "slate." This form does not have an attached keyboard. These systems are designed for mobility, and the exclusion of a keyboard reduces the size and weight of the device. For these reasons, slates typically exclude integrated optical drives. Slates also come in a variety of sizes with diagonal screen measurements ranging from approximately 8 to 15 inches, with most slates in the 10- to 12-inch range.

For extended use at a desk, slates can be docked to a traditional monitor, keyboard, and base station. Slates have grown in popularity in a number of vertical applications, such as field sales, field service, and health care. For outdoor use in the field, slates are also available in a "ruggedized" package. These systems are designed to withstand impacts, drops, wet conditions, and extreme temperature ranges. They also have a screen that is viewable in direct sunlight. (Most tablet displays are designed only for indoor viewing.) The degree of ruggedness is usually reported in terms of military standards. For example, MIL-STD 810 requires the device to withstand repeated three-foot drops onto plywood over concrete and function in wind-blown rain, with a rain rate of four inches per hour. Rugged slates are generally larger, heavier, and more expensive than slates designed for indoor use.

FIGURE 1.2. | A ruggedized slate tablet PC

Convertible

The convertible tablet PC resembles a traditional notebook computer. However, its screen can twist and rotate so that the display can fold down over the keyboard, facing out. A convertible is a best-of-both-worlds computer—it is a traditional notebook computer that can be folded to create a slate-like tablet PC.

By definition, a convertible must include an attached keyboard. However, some systems feature a detachable keyboard that enables the machine to convert into a true slate.

Convertible tablet PCs range in size from 9 to 15 inches, measured diagonally across the screen, with most devices in the 12- to 14-inch range. To reduce weight and increase portability, many convertibles also exclude integrated optical drives.

Computer manufacturers are currently producing more convertibles than slates. In 2007, Hewlett-Packard, Lenovo, and Toshiba produced only convertibles, while Fujitsu and smaller manufacturers such as Motion Computing and TabletKiosk produced slates.

FIGURE 1.3. | A convertible tablet PC

UMPC—Ultra Mobile PC

An Ultra Mobile PC, or UMPC, is a small tablet PC designed to fit into pockets or small bags. Previously known at Microsoft as the Origami Project, UMPCs range in size from a notepad to a paperback book. They generally have touch- or pen-enabled screens that are 7 inches or smaller. The smallest devices have approximately 5-inch screens and weigh around one pound. Some UMPCs are slates while others feature small keyboards intended for thumb typing.

UMPCs versus PDAs

UMPCs are not the same as Personal Digital Assistants (PDAs). PDAs typically run an operating system that is different from that of a desktop computer. Likewise, the applications each uses are usually incompatible. Even so, data stored on a PDA can be synchronized with data on a desktop computer. Popular touch screen PDAs today include the Palm line of hand-held devices and Apple's iPhone.

Like a normal tablet PC, a UMPC is a regular computer that can run the same or similar software found on a full-sized notebook. However, UMPCs generally feature slower processors than found on a larger tablet. Its small form factor also eliminates features such as integrated optical drives and numerous ports.

Since UMPCs place a high emphasis on mobility, many of these devices include built-in support for wireless WAN networking, such as WiMAX or third generation EV-DO cellular networks. Several new UMPC models are planned for release in 2008 and Intel has announced plans to develop a chip specifically designed for small devices (Tan, 2007).

FIGURE 1.4. | The iPAQ 111 Classic Handheld is an example of a UMPC.

Other Input Devices

Tablet PC technology is not limited to notebook-style computers and handheld devices. For schools and districts wanting to use digital inking technology, but cannot replace their existing computers, many upgrade solutions already exist. These solutions include devices that can be connected to standard PCs, thus transforming them into tablet PCs; as well as integrated projection systems that enable teachers to present information while students, from their seats, interact with that same information.

USB-Connected Pen Tablets

Pen tablets are light and portable tablets that allow pen input, but do not provide display capabilities. The pen tablets connect to a regular laptop or PC using a USB interface, providing tablet-like interaction while using a computer that does not otherwise have this capability.

Its operation is simple: users write on the pad-like board at their side and watch their input on a screen. The size of a pen tablet ranges from 4-by-5 inches to 12-by-19 inches.

As of 2007, the most notable maker of pen tablets, Wacom, has two versions available: Intuos and Graphire. These devices are considerably cheaper than standard tablet PCs and provide pen-input and pressure data.

Taking this idea in another direction, Smart Technologies created a wireless USB pen tablet, called Airliner. Unlike the Wacom pen tablets, Airliner technology allows multiple pen-tablet users to write, at the same time, onto a single interactive whiteboard.

Larger Displays

Although the focus of this book is on tablet PCs, there are many instances in an education environment when larger displays are useful. Larger displays are, of course, less portable than their tablet PC counterparts, but they are beneficial in three important circumstances:

- Where tablet PCs remain fixed, such that they are shared among many different classes and students;

- Where the instructor wants to present materials to an entire class; and

- Where the material presented requires a large drawing space and/or greater visibility to the students.

Large Drawing Screens

A large drawing screen is ideal for school computer labs, and it can work nicely as a second monitor in a dual-monitor setup. The screen can be rotated, inclined, and/or removed for lap use.

For example, Wacom's Cintiq 21UX drawing tablet provides a 21.3-inch high-resolution display, and it connects to any computer through a USB interface to provide pen position, pressure, and tilt data.

Multi-Touch PCs

A multi-touch PC allows multiple users to simultaneously manipulate objects on the screen by touch. An example of this technology is Microsoft Surface, which is a tabletop PC that projects a computer image from below to the surface of the table. Once gathered around the table, multiple users can write, gesture, and collaborate on a project.

This technology can have collaborative and educational applications for small groups of students. It is expected to be available near the end of 2007 for approximately $10,000. Multi-touch PCs are not currently available in smaller form factors (such as a slate or convertible).

Interactive Whiteboards

Like an old school chalkboard or grease-pen whiteboard, an interactive whiteboard is a large display device. It is useful for instructors who wish to present information to students as a class. Using an interactive whiteboard, the instructor essentially projects a computer display from a PC to a large pen-input display.

One such display is the popular SMART Board. SMART Boards come in three basic styles: front projection, rear projection, and overlay.

The whiteboard overlay sits on top of an LCD (liquid crystal display) panel and provides a pen-enabled display of up to 60 inches. Because they function through the use of an overlay, there is a gap (about one-inch) between the pen tip and the pen mark.

Slightly less expensive than overlays, rear-projected whiteboard displays provide a 66-inch, pen-enabled screen with no gap between the pen tip and ink projection. These whiteboards include an integrated projector and can be mobile or installed in a permanent location.

As the least expensive version, front-projected SMART interactive whiteboards can be used with existing computers and projectors. They also feature larger display areas than the others.

SMART interactive whiteboard technology allows for the use of any writing implement, including a finger. This technology also features special software that utilizes the pen as either a mouse-input device or as a tool that can lay ink on top of the viewed image—such that the input information is not relayed to the underlying applications.

Benefits of Using Interactive Whiteboards

Recent research on pen-based instruction shows that lessons taught with the aid of interactive whiteboards provide three key benefits:

1. Brighter and clearer presentation of material.

2. Stepped learning and the ability to recall earlier material.

3. Rapid responses to interactive examples so that learning is reinforced or revised.

   (SMART Technologies, 2006; Glover 2005)

Other research has shown interactive whiteboards to:

- Support students with many different learning styles, including students with hearing and visual impairments.

- Raise the level of student engagement in a classroom.

- Streamline teacher preparation.

- Reduce start-up time for digitally-enhanced lessons.

- Motivate teachers to include digital resources.

   (SMART Technologies, 2006)

SMART interactive whiteboards do not come without disadvantages. For example, they currently do not relay pen pressure or tilt information to software applications, meaning they can only send simple mouse events. However, when students are provided with pen tablets (such as the Airliner), chalkboard and overhead displays pale by comparison in terms of their potential for student engagement.

Promethean, a popular interactive learning technology provider, offers another interactive whiteboard system. Promethean Activboard, an interactive whiteboard, can be combined with a computer and Promethean Activote, a Personal Response System (PRS). The PRS, a "clicker" that resembles a small remote control, can be passed out to each student. The buttons on the PRS allow students to answer multiple-choice or true-or-false questions. A question can be posed on the computer, projected on the screen, and each student can answer via the PRS. Statistics on how all students voted can be displayed back to the class. The data displayed to the class is anonymous, although the students' names and a record of how they voted is stored on the computer for later analysis by the teacher.

Tablet PC Software

Even though a tablet PC is essentially a notebook computer, it nonetheless requires special software to run its pen-based functionality. This special software begins with the computer's operating system.

> For a discussion of tablet PC software related to personal productivity, see the section "The Tablet PC: A Personal Productivity Enhancement Tool" in chapter 4.

Microsoft Windows

Microsoft fully supports tablet PCs and has released the Windows XP Tablet PC Edition and the Windows Vista operating systems. Both operating systems feature handwriting recognition. However, handwriting recognition is improved in Windows Vista, and only Windows Vista can learn to recognize an individual user's handwriting.

> For a more detailed look at this software, see the section "Software Features: The Power of the Pen" in chapter 4.

Linux

Many distributions of the Linux operating system can also be installed on a tablet PC. However, users may be required to install additional drivers to support the use of a pen and other hardware. Free and open source applications such as Jarnal (www.dklevine.com/general/software/tc1000/jarnal.htm) are available for taking notes and sketching.

Mac OS X

As of 2007, Apple Computer has not released a tablet Macintosh computer. However, Axiotron and One World Computing have announced an after-market modification that converts a MacBook into a slate. Their solution, the Modbook, replaces the normal display with a Wacom digitizer. It was expected to be available in the second half of 2007.

Handwriting recognition on the Modbook is possible using Apple's Inkwell technology. Originally intended for use with external graphics tablets, Inkwell works equally well with an on-screen digitizer. This technology allows a user to write anywhere on the screen. This writing is converted to text that is then inserted into the active application. Inkwell is also able to process written commands and includes an InkPad application that can be used to handwrite sketches or notes.

At the time of this writing, relatively few pen-enabled applications exist on the Mac OS X platform, compared to the Windows platform.

Windows Applications

Many applications provide their own support for inking (beyond what is provided by the operating system). For some of these applications there is no need to translate handwriting into text—the application can operate entirely in the domain of the digital ink.

> For more information about tablet PC software in a classroom context, see chapter 4, "Personal Productivity for Classroom Teachers."

Microsoft Office

The Microsoft Office suite of products, starting with Office 2003, include built-in support for ink. With a tablet PC, a user can annotate Word files in ink. Users can also write on PowerPoint slides in both the design and delivery phases of a presentation.

Outlook

Although very usable on a tablet PC, Outlook currently does not have full support for ink (even so, ink can be used in e-mail, tasks, and calendar items). Office 2007 promises a fully pen-enabled utility, bringing it productivity benefits comparable to similar applications listed here.

Microsoft Journal

Microsoft Journal is a fully pen-enabled application (it is the ink equivalent of Notepad). Each Journal file is analogous to a notepad of paper, but in this case the notepad is stored digitally. The application allows users to write, erase, copy, and paste ink. Users can also select from a variety of pen styles, including different line colors and widths.

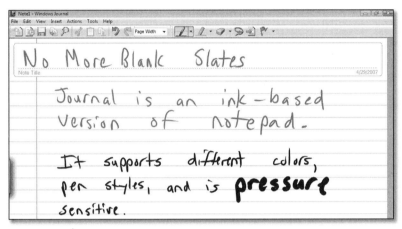

FIGURE 1.5. | Microsoft Journal in action

More sophisticated applications that extend the functionality of Microsoft Journal include Microsoft OneNote, EverNote, and Agilix GoBinder.

Ink-Enabled Software

Microsoft Office OneNote. A digital notebook.
   http://office.microsoft.com/en-us/onenote/

Microsoft PowerToys for Windows XP Tablet PC Edition. This is a group of programs designed to enhance the tablet PC experience.
   www.microsoft.com/windowsxp/downloads/powertoys/tabletpc.mspx

EverNote. A software application that allows users to capture text notes, images, digital ink, and more.
   www.evernote.com

StrokeIt. An advanced mouse gesture-recognition engine that lets users "draw" on their computer screen using a mouse.
www.tcbmi.com/strokeit/

MindManager. A visually-oriented information mapping software.
www.mindjet.com

Inspiration and Kidspiration. A graphics-oriented mapping software designed for K–5 learners.
www.inspiration.com

PDF Annotator. A software that allows users to annotate any PDF file using the mouse or a tablet PC pen.
www.ograhl.com/en/pdfannotator/

Adaptive Book Project. The tablet PC version of this project lets users create, organize, and share pen-based annotations.
www.cs.cmu.edu/~ab/

Windows Messenger. This instant messaging software supports ink within messages.
www.microsoft.com/windowsxp/using/windowsmessenger/

Trillian Astra. Like Windows Messenger, this instant messaging software also supports ink within messages.
www.trillian.im/

Course and Content Management

Moodle. A free, open source software package designed to help educators create effective online learning communities.
http://moodle.org

Sakai. A set of software tools designed to help instructors and students collaborate and communicate.
http://sakaiproject.org

GoCourse Learning System. An instructional and course management system.
www.agilix.com/GoCourse.aspx

GoBinder. A personal productivity application for students and professionals.
www.agilix.com/GoBinder.aspx

Blackboard Backpack. An electronic content management tool.
http://backpack.blackboard.com

Thinkwell. A producer of online textbooks and other interactive electronic courseware.
www.thinkwell.com

Elluminate. A real-time virtual classroom environment designed for distance education and collaboration with academic institutions.
www.elluminate.com

Adobe Connect. A flexible Web communication system, designed to help users create and manage e-learning courses and curricula.
www.adobe.com/products/connect/

FranklinCovey PlanPlus Online. An electronic version of this popular planning system.
http://planplusonline.com

Sketching Software: General

ScanScribe. A document image editor that allows users to manipulate sketches, handwritten notes, whiteboard images, screenshots, and scanned documents.
http://scanscribe.com

Geometer's Sketchpad. This software allows users to build and investigate mathematical models, objects, figures, diagrams, and graphs.
www.dynamicgeometry.com

Winplot. A general-purpose plotting utility that allows users to draw curves and surfaces.
http://math.exeter.edu/rparris/winplot.html

LaTeX. A document markup language and preparation system that automates many typesetting and desktop publishing tasks.
www.latex-project.org/intro.html

Sketching Software: Art and Music

ArtRage. A software that provides a simple blank canvas and a set of brushes, pens, and other tools that allow for complete freedom of expression.
www.ambientdesign.com/artrage.html

CorelDRAW. A popular graphics program that provides excellent pressure sensitivity and drawing capabilities.
http://coreldraw.com

Paint.NET. A free image and photo editing software.
www.getpaint.net

LADDER Sheet Music. A software that will allow users to score musical notes and replay them.
http://srl.csdl.tamu.edu/musicscribble.shtml
http://srl.csdl.tamu.edu/posters/SRMusicPoster.ppt

Sketching Software: Math and Science

FluidMath. A software that allows instructors to write equations and draw diagrams or objects. Equations are recognized mathematically and can be graphed using a special gesture with a tablet PC pen.
www.fluidmath.com

ChemPad. A software that translates standard two-dimensional drawings of molecules into three-dimensional structures.
http://graphics.cs.brown.edu/research/chempad/home.html

MathPad2. A mathematical sketching software that converts handwritten math formulas into free-form diagrams.
www.cs.brown.edu/~jjl/mathpad/

xThink MathJournal. A software that attempts to simplify mathematical formatting on the computer.
www.xthink.com

Recording Software

Camtasia Studio. Camtasia is a screen-recording software. Though not designed for use exclusively with tablet PCs, this software is designed to record on-screen activity. Camtasia's screen capture feature can record the instructor's pen interaction with presentation slides. Accompanying audio explanations can also be recorded. Students can then access these recordings for step-by-step review.
www.techsmith.com/camtasia/

Other similar PC-based screen recording software includes Adobe Captivate (www.adobe.com/products/captivate/) and My Screen Recorder Pro (www.deskshare.com/msrpro.aspx).

Collaboration Software

Tablet PC software applications specifically designed to enhance classroom collaboration constitute a small but growing segment of the software market. The applications highlighted here can provide profoundly positive classroom experiences for teachers and students alike.

DyKnow Vision. Designed for use on tablet PCs, interactive whiteboards, and non-tablet PCs, DyKnow Vision is collaborative note-taking software. Teachers can use this software to transmit their presentations to student computers for their annotation. Students can use the tools in this software to respond to a lesson in real time; then later replay that lesson step-by-step. This fully supported, scalable software is designed to work in fixed, mobile, and distance learning environments.

www.dyknow.com

Classroom Presenter. Classroom Presenter is software that integrates computer-generated slides and digital ink and then synchronizes those files on multiple computers. The result is a flexible, interactive learning environment where both instructor and students alike can write on a given slide in real time. Teachers receive a list of student submissions and can choose which submissions to display to the class. Moreover, teachers can lock student input to only the slide currently being worked on, or they can unlock the slides to allow students to browse ahead or go back for review.

http://classroompresenter.cs.washington.edu

Ubiquitous Presenter. Similar to Classroom Presenter, this tablet PC software enables teachers to annotate prepared class presentation slides in real time. The software then allows students to synchronize with the respective lesson and interact with the materials in real time. Conversely, student computers can be unsynchronized to the lesson, thus allowing students to view the presentation slides at will. The instructor's inking is archived online, stroke-by-stroke, and students can access and replay the lesson at any time.

http://up.ucsd.edu/about/WhatIsUP.html

2 Simpler Is Better

BREAKING THE KEYBOARD PARADIGM

DAVID S. SWEENEY
    Director for Information Technology
    Division of Student Affairs
    Texas A&M University

For all their coolness, tablet PCs incorporate some old ideas. The form of the tablet, which dates back to Mesopotamia, was small enough to be relatively portable, even when made out of stone.

FIGURE 2.1 | Set in stone, pressed into wax, or digitally "inked" onto a screen, pictures and words written on tablets have helped to define knowledge and experience throughout human history.

"Inking" is intrinsically personal. Handwriting can communicate more about a person than typewritten text. Despite the advent of the keyboard and mouse, the act of writing with an instrument such as a stylus or pen remains the preferred method of written communication for most, primarily because it is so natural and intuitive. In fact, the first typewriters, with their QWERTY keyboards, were not designed to be intuitive but to facilitate the act of typing without jamming the mechanical strikers.

In other words, although keyboards can provide an efficient way to write text, the keyboard itself was not designed to be intuitive or necessarily efficient. Since its inception, the keyboard has gone through many variations, including those with altered key placement and "more efficient" models entering the market, but these specialty items remain the exception. The QWERTY keyboard (at least in the western hemisphere) has withstood the test of time, in large part because it came along—and became the standard—at the right time. The rise of tablet PCs in many ways represents a return to a simpler method of communicating written language. Tablet PCs, too, may be coming along at the right time and could very well become the new standard for written communication.

Keyboards, in and of themselves, are not very good at creating graphics. Progress has been made in the way of mouse-driven drawing tools and programs, but it could be argued that these new developments are only workarounds designed to merely mimic the basic movements of drawing by hand. By contrast, using nothing more than a stylus and an inking program, tablet PC users can write text and draw a diagram within the same document. These digital ink bits are called annotations. More traditional software programs, such as word processing and graphics packages, don't have annotations. Once again, the advanced technology of the tablet PC is, in essence, a return to a simpler form of written communication. Some of the newer tablet PC drawing programs even have pressure-sensitive features that allow the user to draw a heavy or light line, just as if a pencil were being used.

In his recent book, *The World is Flat,* Thomas Friedman (2006) hypothesizes that technology has leveled or "flattened" the global playing field. This flattening has happened as a result of what Friedman calls the "triple convergence" of platform, process, and people. In a nutshell, when an innovative platform takes hold, processes that use the platform must change. If the right people are available, trained, and become adept in this technology and process paradigm, they become the third prong of the triple convergence.

The question has been asked, "If the tablet is merely digital paper, why not just use real paper and save electricity?" It's an interesting question, but one that actually misses the point. A tablet PC isn't "merely" digital paper. Although tablet PCs utilize a traditional method of written communication, they also let users communicate ideas without stamps or envelopes. Moreover, because tablet PCs use digital ink, users can deliver all of their work digitally, almost instantly, to thousands of people just as easily as to one, and at a fraction of the cost. This supports Friedman's idea of the "flattening of communication."

Communication Technology Itself Is Not Communication

As "connected" as we are, people can feel increasingly disconnected from each other, partially as a result of technology use. My greatest fear as a technology professional, educator, and parent is that we will continue to increase our level of technical connectivity in a futile effort to feel more socially connected, and yet the end result will be that we feel increasingly isolated from each other. In a sense, technology itself feeds the hunger that it creates, but only with empty calories. In a very real way, educators have an essential role to play in preventing this disconnect.

There was a time, not that long ago, when news traveled only as fast as a horse. President Jefferson didn't know that Lewis and Clark were successful in their 1804–1806 expedition until they were well on their way back home. Fast-forward roughly 200 years—I grew up in the age of television news but never really liked it, choosing instead to gather my news mostly through the newspaper. There's something about the permanency of print, the feel of the pages as you fold back the "A" section to read the editorials on the back page. This way of reading has always appealed to me in a romantic way. My kids have learned through my example to appreciate the newspaper, to a point. Today's young people communicate more through texting and instant messaging than through newspapers or even e-mail.

Which is to say, kids today get their news much more quickly and by less permanent means. Although mobile phones are in common use, college-age students say they use their phones almost as much for text messaging as for voice communication. A recent survey revealed that 99% of students at a particular higher-education institution had mobile phones (Student Life Studies, 2007); while on a national level 63% of Americans aged 18 to 27 use text messaging. The percentages decrease as age increases, thus lending credence to Friedman's triple-convergence hypothesis—specifically, that young people today are more prepared to operate efficiently in this wired and wireless world. Voice-over IP (VoIP) telecommunication services such as Skype are more popular by the day. Young people expect instant communication, and tablet PCs allow them to communicate instantly through a medium in which they are already familiar.

All of this brings up the element of collaboration. Tablet PCs (and all computers with Internet access, for that matter) allow users to move beyond mere communication and into the realm of an interactive community, where capital is measured in the currency of ideas. Participation in this community is the ultimate "flattener." No longer is a participant or an idea limited by time or distance—users can connect from around the world just as easily as they can from across the room. Tablet PCs can be used to great advantage in a collaborative environment, and collaborative tools (yet another Friedman flattener) have been developed specifically for tablet PCs that take advantage of the many beneficial characteristics of stylus computing.

Recall, if you will, the core of Friedman's argument: When an innovative platform takes hold, the processes and people that use the platform must change. The resulting environment can be truly innovative. This is, in essence, the story of the tablet PC. The microcomputer (morphed into the tablet PC) is the innovative platform; the people are the younger generation among us; and the process is the changing way we view what technology is and what it can do for us. The tablet PC is the natural result of a convergence of some very old and very new technologies.

TABLET PCS IN THE REAL WORLD

Personal Computing Made Personal

"Dad, where's the tablet?"

Luke, my 6 year old, asks me this question at least twice a day. Once he locates it, he is off to the races, quickly browsing to a highly frenetic and animated Web site with lots of bouncy characters, or he's launching the latest game he's been working on.

Kathryn, my 12 year old, patiently waits her turn so she can check her e-mail, look up the latest video on YouTube, or check out how the latest episode of her podcast sounds. Austin, my 8 year old, is perhaps more resourceful. Rather than wait his turn, he walks next door to use his grandfather's wireless laptop to check his e-mail or look for a Wikipedia story on copperhead snakes. Hannah, who is 7, would make sure I heard about it if she did not spend at least part of the day looking for horse resources on the Web. Her latest find is a Web site that lets you adopt and take care of a horse, all virtually, of course.

All of them are just as comfortable using a stylus as a mouse. In fact, I've observed that they are better at using the on-screen keyboard than the physical one. One of the curious things about all of these "techno-kids" is that they wouldn't be caught dead using the fully serviceable desktop in the bedroom—they simply don't see why they should use a computer with wires. Wires are not part of their paradigm. But there is more to it than that. They see computers very differently from the way I see them.

I've been using tablet PCs since 2002. In the beginning, using a tablet PC was a novelty. A personal computer in book form. A new gizmo high on the "cool" scale. I imagined a twinkle in my smiling eyes while carrying my sleek tablet through the office. But my initial experience with tablets was not always stellar. Back in those days, inking was not as effective as it is now, nor was handwriting recognition particularly impressive.

Tablet PCs were relatively heavy, and battery life was not long. Mobile processors were just catching on, and available models were expensive and slow. I had a top-of-the-line model with an 800-megahertz processor, 20 gigabytes of disk space, and 512 megabytes of memory. Any dreams in those days of using that first model as a primary computer were out of the question—there simply wasn't enough power. I longed for the day when a tablet PC could serve as my primary machine and thus eliminate the need for a desktop computer. I thought that going totally mobile would be the ultimate in geek heaven. That day came sooner than I thought.

In 2005, I bought a tablet PC with a 1.8 gigahertz processor, 1 gigabyte of memory, 6 hours of battery life and 160 gigabytes of disk space. I still use it today as my primary computer for both work and school. I use it to take notes during meetings, check e-mail, write programs, browse the Web, conduct research, show presentations, record podcasts, and listen to music. I use my tablet in the boardroom, the classroom, on airplanes, on the kitchen table, and on my lap in bed at the end of the day. I use it in a variety of ways: with a wireless Bluetooth keyboard and mouse; docked on my desk at work with a large secondary monitor and a comfortable roller-ball mouse; and with nothing more than a stylus to take notes during class and meetings. I connect to the Internet equally well with wire or without. As an information technology professional, I have always needed both a desktop and a laptop, but not anymore.

For all the functionality I have wrung out of my tablet, I still view it as a fancy, mobile computer. My paradigm is based on what the tablet can *do*. But here's the rub: My kids base their paradigm on what the tablet *is*: a means to knowledge, communication, and even community. What has taken me most of my professional life to understand, they get intuitively.

3 | Key Resources

Many key tablet PC resources are mentioned in this book. They are gathered in this chapter for easy reference.

Software

Classroom Presenter. A collaboration software that allows instructors to deliver a presentation and to facilitate class interaction.

http://classroompresenter.cs.washington.edu

DyKnow Vision. A flexible and interactive collaborative note-taking software.

www.dyknow.com

Microsoft PowerToys for Windows XP Tablet PC Edition. A downloadable collection of free programs for the tablet PC.

www.microsoft.com/windowsxp/downloads/
powertoys/tabletpc.mspx

Microsoft Windows XP Tablet PC Homepage. The starting point for Microsoft software information and downloads.
www.microsoft.com/windowsxp/tabletpc/

Tablet PC Post. A clearing house for tablet PC software.
www.tabletpcpost.com

Ubiquitous Presenter. A collaboration software that allows users to annotate prepared class presentation slides in real time.
http://up.ucsd.edu

Technical Support

1-to-1 Learning: Laptop Programs that Work. This popular book shows readers how to plan and roll out a 1-to-1 laptop program that will work from day one.
www.iste.org/laptop/

Gartner "Magic Quadrant for Global Enterprise Notebook PCs." A leading information technology research and advisory company published this helpful document. To view product information, go the following URL and search for "Magic Quadrant."
www.gartner.com

HP K–12 Education. Hewlett-Packard's end-to-end technology solutions for K–12 education.
www.hp.com/go/k12/

Meru Networks. A technology developer that purports to overcome the current limitations of high-volume, multi-user wireless network environments.
www.merunetworks.com

Tablet PC Buying Guide. An online guide designed to help users select the best product for their needs.
www.hp.com/sbso/buyguides/pg_tablet_pcs.html

Technology Questions. An online "community of technology enthusiasts" that focuses on technology and includes forums for answering questions about tablet PC computing.
www.technologyquestions.com

Conferences

The ISTE Institute. A professional-development program designed for teams of educators who are focused on increasing their effectiveness on student learning through the integration of technology.

www.iste.org/content/navigationmenu/professional_development/
iste_institute/iste_institute.htm

The Laptop Institute. Hosted each summer by the Lausanne Collegiate School in Memphis, Tennessee, this annual event brings together upwards of 500 participants from K–12 schools that have, or are considering, a 1-to-1 mobile PC deployment.

www.laptopinstitute.com

NECC. National Education Computing Conference. The most comprehensive educational technology event in the world.

http://center.uoregon.edu/ISTE/

Pen-Based Learning Technologies (PLT). A conference devoted to understanding the relationships among pen-based interfaces and pedagogy, learning tasks, and learning settings.

http://plt2007.ing.unict.it

"Tablets in the Classroom" Conference. Hosted three or four times each year by the Cincinnati Country Day School, this thoroughly hands-on event focuses exclusively on 1-to-1 tablet PC deployments.

www.countryday.net/academics/technology_tablet.aspx

Workshop on the Impact of Pen-based Technology in Education (WIPTE). Held annually at Purdue University, this event covers K–12 and higher education deployments of tablet PCs and other pen-based computing approaches.

www.purdue.edu/wipte

Assessment Resources

SRI International Guidebook. Supporting the evaluation of technology-based course redesign projects, this guidebook helps educators design and conduct an evaluation of the learning gains they achieve in their own classrooms.

http://ctl.sri.com/projects/displayProject.jsp?Nick=hpguide

The Student Tablet PC. Although its focus is on higher education, this site is nonetheless an excellent source for information on tablet PC use for all students.

www.studenttabletpc.com

Tablet PC In-Service

IN THIS SECTION

Many believe the tablet PC to be the device that can transform teaching and learning. But before students can benefit, educators must become comfortable with this technology.

The chapters in Part II provide a practical guide for using tablet PCs to instruct, communicate, and collaborate both in and out of the classroom. Also included in this section are examples and case studies taken from real teachers in real classrooms, as well as advice for deploying tablet PCs at the district level.

4 Personal Productivity

FOR CLASSROOM TEACHERS

MARK PAYTON
   IT Director
   Vermont Academy

IN THIS CHAPTER

- What personal productivity means

- The tablet PC and enhanced personal productivity

- Improved productivity with tablet PC software: task, time, information management, and more

- Case studies: Vermont Academy, Colorado School for the Deaf and the Blind

- Challenges and future directions

The combination of portability, power, and pen allows the tablet PC to be a first rate personal productivity tool for both students and teachers.

Does personal productivity have any meaning in the classroom or other instructional situations? If we accept that "improved productivity" means doing things better, faster, and more efficiently, then, yes, it does.

The Problem with Personal Productivity

The term "personal" is significant. Ask any number of people what it means to be "more productive" and you will likely get as many varied answers as you have individuals.

To a student, increasing efficiency might include the ability to easily and accurately track assignments and their due dates; have ready access to the source materials required to complete those assignments; quickly locate class notes (and, as importantly, specific information in those notes); and make contact with a classmate or teacher via instant messaging (IM), an Internet phone service (e.g., Skype), or e-mail.

To a faculty member, however, improving personal productivity might instead include the ability to have ready access to an accurate and current calendar of class, department, and other meetings; ensure that lesson plans and materials (not to mention upgraded assignments) are always available; and maintain on-demand access to the current course documents and grade books.

With previous technologies, the terms "ready-access" and "on-demand" were more associated with filing cabinets in an office; books, planners, and folders filled with paper; or with files kept on a desktop computer.

Even with the advent of notebook computers, wireless Internet access, and electronic planners, access to information was—and is—still limited to the design of the respective notebook computer in question. Although notebook computers are great tools, they lack a certain dynamic flexibility. Traditional notebooks offer only a single input method (keyboard and mouse) and require a flat-surface workspace, be it a table top, a lap, or the floor.

The method for many on-the-go people who need to manage appointments and remember special days (students and classroom teachers among them) is a kind of hybrid approach. In addition to depending on notebook computers, many people often use a Day Runner or some other paper-based management system (such as a pile of folders, binders, or spiral notebooks stuffed into a backpack).

However organized or efficient this hybrid method, it often involves a lot of repeated effort, as tasks must be manually copied, crossed off, and forwarded on a daily basis. What's more, documents can be easily misplaced or damaged. Part of improving personal productivity means having quick and easy access to any piece of information. When a person takes many minutes to hunt for a document that only turns up damaged or missing, then that person is neither being efficient nor productive.

This is only to say that both an organized system and a means of searching for and locating specific information within that system are important for optimal productivity. What's more, being limited to a single location or system (an office with filing cabinets, for example) can also be a significant constraint on productivity.

What to do? Pick up a tablet PC.

A Personal Productivity Enhancement Tool

What follows is a discussion of the tablet PC's many benefits, including portability, flexibility, the advantages of pen-input technology, and more.

Portability

Tablet PCs generally fall into the sub-notebook or ultra-portable category. Full size slate-style tablet PCs are often a mere 11 mm in thickness and weigh as little as two pounds. Most tablet PCs weigh somewhat more than that, but even convertible models with keyboards are generally in the 3- to 4-pound range.

As light as they are, these computers still commonly offer a 12.1-inch screen, though screen sizes can vary anywhere from 8.4 to 14 inches. Generally, the weight varies in direct proportion to the screen size.

> For a more detailed discussion of the technical aspects of tablet PCs, please see "The Tablet PC: A Machine for Every Occasion" in chapter 1.

This light weight makes the tablet PC easy to carry and fit into a large bag, backpack, or briefcase. It is available when and where you need it. Imagine the impact on your productivity when your to-do list, calendar, contacts list, current working documents, and reference documents are always at the ready.

Flexibility

Like many sub-notebook computers, most tablet PCs come with some sort of docking system that allows users to create a functional desktop computer replacement (Fig. 4.1).

Adding an external monitor to the docking station allows users to use Windows' extended desktop to see two full screens at once. Different applications can run on each desktop screen and items can be dragged and dropped between them. This is a useful way to work on documents while having hand-written notes or other source materials always visible.

It is difficult to overstate the benefits of the extended desktop to students and faculty. Reference materials (either from handwritten notes, files, or from the Internet) can be displayed on one screen, while the working document remains displayed on the other. Both cut-and-paste and drag-and-drop are enabled between the screens, and users can convert handwriting into text on the fly.

FIGURE 4.1. | When a tablet PC is docked, a full-size keyboard, mouse, DVD drive, and second monitor can be connected.

Likewise, the docking station can keep a full-size keyboard, mouse, wired network connection, printer, and other peripherals always attached. This allows for a docked tablet PC to act and feel just like a desktop system. Today's dual core chips provide plenty of power for most desktop tasks and run at full speed while docked, while running in low-power mode at other times.

When not docked, users still have the full use of the notebook computer wherever they would normally use one, be it a library carrel, kitchen table, or coffee shop.

Where tablet PCs come into their own, however, is when they are running in tablet mode rather than in notebook mode (or with a keyboard attached if it is a slate model). As tablets, they can be used when users are standing up; lying down; sitting in a car, bus, subway, or train; and even while walking. Because they can be held much like a book in this mode, reading is much more enjoyable on a tablet PC than on other types of computers. While tablet mode isn't ideal for generating long documents, quick e-mail messages and instant messages can be created (such as those handwritten in Windows Messenger and Trillian, which itself can connect to multiple IM services). Moreover, notes in Microsoft Journal or OneNote, or documents in Microsoft Word, PowerPoint, and Excel can be marked up and annotated.

Lectures and Instruction

Tablet PCs bring many presentation benefits and productivity enhancements to a classroom teacher. For instructors who use many supporting documents or references, the tablet PC offers them the ability to keep all of their materials in one place and readily available (and not easily be lost, misplaced, or forgotten). Because of the tablet form itself, these materials can be available, for example, while standing at a podium, seated at a desk, or walking around the classroom.

Often, teachable moments occur outside the classroom (for example, when a student stops the instructor in the hallway to ask a question). With all of the class materials literally in hand, not to mention an endless supply of blank "paper" with multiple pens and markers, a teacher with a tablet PC is poised to take advantage of these times and make them maximally productive. If the student has a tablet PC and OneNote, a shared session can even be created on the spot to allow the two to work together on the same work space.

The ability to make wireless presentations has profound ramifications for productivity as well. The tablet PC coupled with a wireless projector allows teachers more direct interaction with the students during a presentation. Not only does this technology combination enable teachers to communicate more effectively, it also lets them easily monitor student behavior.

For more information about wireless projectors and interactive whiteboards, see "Other Input Devices" (p. 21) and "Larger Displays" (p. 22) in chapter 1.

Pen Input

Pen input is the most obvious element that makes the tablet PC what it is. With it, you can take notes into ink-enabled applications such as OneNote or Journal, make on-screen drawings in applications such as ArtRage, and interact with Web- and text-based applications. You can also take advantage of the extended features in ink-aware applications such as Word and PowerPoint, and even interact with Windows itself in a more direct fashion than would be normally possible with a mouse alone.

> For an overview of tablet PC software, see "Tablet PC Software" in chapter 1. For more about tablet PC software as they relate to personal productivity, see "Software Features: The Power of the Pen" in this chapter.

Particularly for younger students, the pen may be a much more comfortable and familiar input device than a keyboard. Indeed, introducing tablet PC pen functionality at the lowest grades can establish pen-input as a normal part of the computing experience (instead of being a perceived foreign element or "latecomer," which it may seem to many). There is still hope for those of us with keyboard and mouse habits firmly ingrained. Many veteran tablet PC users report that, while first getting used to pen-input, they found it extremely helpful to avoid the keyboard for an extended period of time. Like with any other activity, proficiency comes with practice, and after a few weeks of pen-only usage, these same traditional users found that they had developed a new appreciation for the usefulness of the pen, as well as a newfound understanding of when to use pen-input and when to use a keyboard.

In lieu of the seemingly drastic step of migrating to pen-only input for all tasks and programs, users can practice developing their pen skills by using selective applications such as ArtRage, or by playing some of the pen-focused games such as Sudoku or the Crossword Puzzle PowerToy. And, of course, finding and regularly using one application that makes excellent use of the pen, such as PlanPlus or OneNote, will help a user to develop the skills and habits necessary for savvy digital ink use.

Built-in Networking (802.11, Bluetooth, IR)

As is common with notebook computers these days, tablet PCs generally come with various types of wireless connectivity. Bluetooth can be used to communicate with headsets for use with Skype, desktop keyboards, mice, and many other peripherals. Infrared can be used to exchange files with other users quickly and easily. 802.11-compatible and mobile broadband networking allow for full wireless Internet access.

Storage Capacity

As disk capacities increase, even while the physical size of disk drives decrease, a tablet PC can carry more and more programs and files. With current disk sizes of around 120 gigabytes readily and inexpensively available, it is quite feasible for users to carry nearly everything they might need or want on a tablet PC.

On my tablet PC, for example, I have my complete calendar and task list, the notes of every meeting I have attended in the last four years, all the documents that I need for reference, my class plans, a library of hundreds of texts, a couple of gigabytes of music and a few videos, my entire set of Internet bookmarks, source code for all of my recent programs, my entire e-mail mailbox—all readily available, wherever I am and whenever I need it.

Always Available

Even teachers who rely heavily on digital content probably still rely on the presence of physical texts, paper, writing utensils, calculators, and the like, to conduct their lessons. But problems sometimes result when teachers or students forget to carry along some of these standard items, and the consequences of this obstacle can range from a minor class disruption to an abrupt change in lesson plans. More and more, however, the tablet PC can function as a digital substitute for these standard physical necessities, thus minimizing—if not eliminating—this problem altogether.

A large and ever-increasing number of texts are available right now. The note-taking tools profiled in this book provide a nearly unlimited supply of virtual paper, pens, and markers. What's more, a number of sophisticated virtual calculators are available, as are many other virtual tools.

Indoor/Outdoor Screens

Indoor/outdoor displays, an option on many (though not all) tablet PCs, enable a tablet's screen to be seen in all but the brightest direct sunlight, further emphasizing the tablet's potential to be used anywhere. Outdoor options include being in the field for data collection and note taking, on the quad or green for leisure or study, or even on the athletic field to reference a playbook or diagram a play.

Battery Life

Although battery life is still an area in need of improvement, current technology is good enough that a teacher or student can get through an entire class day without access to electrical power or an extended battery. With mindful power management, users can put many tablet PCs into standby—without closing their applications—while they swap their spent batteries for fresh ones. Between charges, this strategy can double the length of a working session. And some tablet PCs have optional larger batteries that allow significantly more time between charges. Still others offer a way of attaching a second battery that can more than double the amount of usable time unplugged.

Software Features: The Power of the Pen

As with any computer, it is ultimately the user's software that determines the usefulness of the system. But when the tablet PC platform was first released in 2002, there was little tablet-PC-specific software available to enhance personal productivity.

As the popularity of the tablet PC platform has grown over the years, the quantity and quality of software—either written or adapted to take advantage of the pen—has increased dramatically. Today, there are many software packages for the tablet PC platform that can help students and teachers to be more productive.

Although personal productivity is perhaps more a concern for older students and faculty, many of the applications described in this section are beneficial for younger students.

For an overview of software for the tablet PC, see "Tablet PC Software" in chapter 1.

Microsoft Windows

The two Windows operating systems that run on tablet PCs (Vista and Windows XP Tablet PC Edition) provide a number of capabilities that allow almost any application to be used with the pen. If an application uses standard Windows controls, such as text boxes, Windows will display the Tablet Input Panel icon (TIP), which, when clicked, will provide a pen-oriented input box. The TIP translates the user's ink strokes into text, which is then placed in the text box. All standard Windows dialog boxes work this way, since the TIP can be activated manually by the user and the text will go to whatever control has input focus. Even applications that use non-standard input controls can be used with the pen.

Vista improves on this integration of the pen with an improved TIP, better handwriting recognition (including personalized recognitions and trainable handwriting recognition), "pen flicks" (programmable pen macros), and the ability to select and manipulate multiple items on the desktop or Explorer window (Fig. 4.2).

Windows XP users can gain the functionality of pen flicks, and much more, with third-party applications such as StrokeIt.

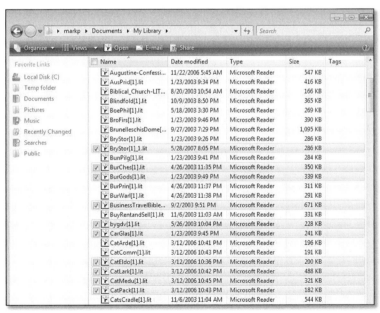

FIGURE 4.2. | With Windows Vista, pen users can now select and manipulate multiple files and objects on the desktop and in Explorer windows.

Windows Vista TIP Tutorial

Using a pen, a user can easily input text into a given Windows application. The user simply taps the text field where one would normally type. The tap brings up an icon that opens a pop-up window called the Tablet PC Input Panel, or TIP. The TIP allows the user to enter handwriting, which is then translated to text. The TIP allows text to be entered in three ways:

1. An entire line of text can be entered and recognized together. Recognized text is shown below the handwriting (in this case, http:\\www.iste.org).

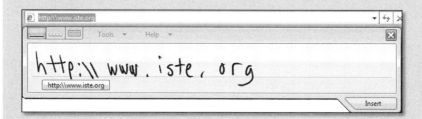

2. Letters can be recognized individually. Individual letter recognition is useful for writing non-English words—individual letters can be easily corrected with a pull-down menu that is provided for each letter.

3. An on-screen keyboard can be tapped by the pen to enter text. The on-screen keyboard provides an easy alternative for anyone familiar with a standard QWERTY keyboard.

(Continued)

Vista's letter recognition can improve as you use it. By using the Handwriting Personalization function, you can manually train it to recognize specific characters or words that are frequently recognized incorrectly.

(Continued)

Vista allows you to customize pen options. For example, eight different "flicks" of the pen can be assigned specific functions within Vista, enabling quick pen access to common functions.

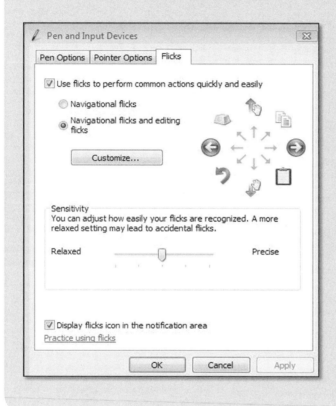

Task, Time, and Information Management

This category of software is essentially the electronic equivalent of a FranklinCovey Day Planner. (Indeed, the software I use in this category is distributed by FranklinCovey, the maker of those planners.) Regardless of brand, software in this category provides some or all of the following: task management, calendar and appointment management, planning and goals management, contact management, and note-taking capabilities.

Software in this category has existed for many years, and any of these management systems should run on Windows XP Tablet PC Edition. Newer tablet PC-oriented options include the commercial packages FranklinCovey PlanPlus (Fig. 4.3), and Agilix GoBinder. GoBinder Lite is distributed free, as part of the Microsoft Tablet PC Education Pack. The feature sets in GoBinder and GoBinder Lite are specifically oriented toward education uses.

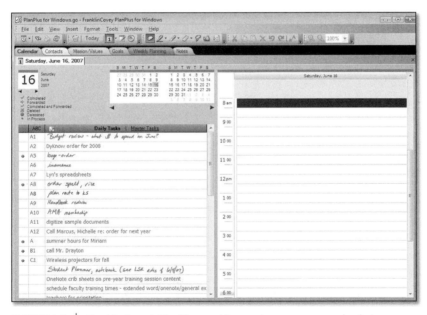

FIGURE 4.3. | FranklinCovey's PlanPlus combines task management, calendaring, notes, and a number of other time-management and planning tools into one package. Agilix GoBinder is similar, visually and functionally.

It is hard to overestimate the productivity benefits that good, consistent use of time- and task-management software can bring. Using tablet PCs, all the benefits of traditional paper systems are carried over to the electronic system, with the added benefits of unlimited space (no monthly page changes or refills to worry about); perpetuity of content (for appointments and tasks in both the past and the future); and full content searching (including those in ink that let you quickly locate all references to your search term without thumbing through thousands of pages).

In addition, these time- and task-management applications create a virtual printer that allows other applications to "print" to note pages within them. These systems also allow for cutting text and pictures from Web sites or other applications and pasting them into note pages.

For schools that use the software Blackboard for course content management, a program called Blackboard Backpack (also written by Agilix; Fig. 4.4) is available, which combines many management features and integrates them into Blackboard. For more information on using Blackboard Backpack, see "Note Taking" (p. 59).

FIGURE 4.4. | This is the task and calendar view in Blackboard Backpack.

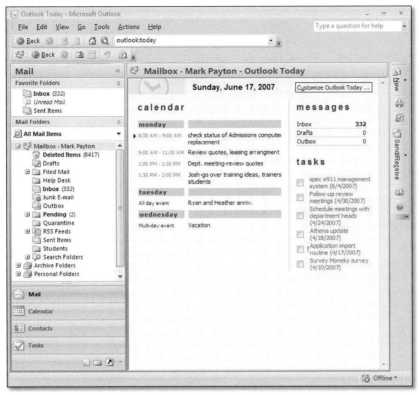

FIGURE 4.5. | Outlook's "Outlook Today" view shows current and upcoming tasks and appointments, as well as a count of unread e-mails at a single glance.

Another option in this category is Microsoft Outlook. Outlook 2007 includes the ability to ink in e-mail messages as well as calendar, contact, and task notes (Fig. 4.5). Unfortunately, inking ability is otherwise minimal for Outlook. However, a third-party add-in called Tablet Enhancements for Outlook (by Einstein Technologies) makes Outlook 2003 or 2007 a fully pen-enabled application.

Note Taking

The applications in this category are generally true ink-enabled applications, though exceptions exist. Nonetheless, this group of programs focuses specifically on the process of note taking and other similar creative processes.

Take Note

Note taking on a tablet PC is one of those activities that is deceptive in its familiarity. It doesn't seem all that different from taking notes in a paper notebook, and it is not until you actually begin to take notes on a tablet PC that you discover the myriad subtle and not-so-subtle productivity improvements this technology delivers.

Using the note-taking applications mentioned here, students can record class notes into their tablet PCs as easily as they can into a paper notebook. In fact, many tasks are even easier. Notes can be color-coded and readily highlighted without the need to keep a bundle of different pens on the desk. Notes can be reorganized on the fly, either through the dragging and dropping of blocks of ink or by inserting space where needed into existing notes. Images and text from Web pages or electronic handouts can be incorporated directly into the notes. Notes can even be made directly onto electronic handouts.

When it comes time to review, specific topics can be quickly found via the search functionality found on tablet PC note-taking software. These digital notes can also be shared with friends while still remaining available to the original author.

Windows Journal

Every Windows-based tablet PC comes with Windows Journal, software that could be characterized as the inkable equivalent of WordPad. Windows Journal is a basic ink-oriented note-taking program that allows users to write, draw, and highlight in multiple colors; work on different backgrounds (including lined and unlined pages and various size grids); and embed pictures and other content from Web pages or other applications. This software even provides a virtual printer with which a user can print from any program and then mark up the output. Because this software stores its content as individual files, documents can be organized via standard Windows file management techniques. Likewise, content is searchable even though it resides as ink. For many users, Windows Journal may be all that is required.

GoBinder, PlanPlus, and Backpack

Note taking is also a feature of GoBinder, PlanPlus, and Backpack. Each uses an internal organizational structure that is independent of Windows' file management system. Text, images, and ink can be combined in notes (Fig. 4.6). Each application installs a virtual printer that allows any printable item to become a note within the normal notebook structure.

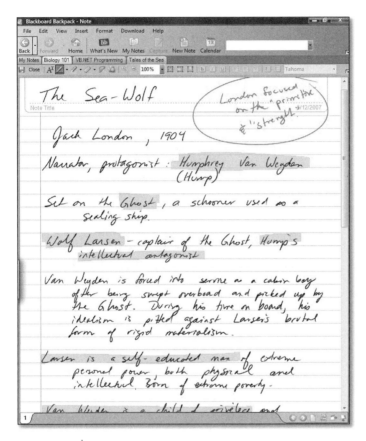

FIGURE 4.6. | This is how notes can look when made in Backpack. Notes taken using GoBinder and PlanPlus are similar in terms of screen layout and capabilities.

Microsoft OneNote

Microsoft OneNote is a capable and feature-rich application. It incorporates a multiple-notebook paradigm into the program itself, meaning that notes are organized in a familiar and intuitive manner (Fig. 4.7). All content is saved automatically as the user works, and all content is easily searchable. Users can select a number of pre-made page designs (e.g., blank, lined, or grids) or create stationery with their own designs.

Should an instructor have students work together, OneNote has a feature called Shared Sessions that allows users to conduct collaborative note-taking sessions. Everyone either sees the notes as they are taken or they can contribute to them in real time.

Using OneNote, students can record audio and video as they take notes, and OneNote will synchronize the recording and the notes. At playback (review) time, students will see the notes highlighted—in sync with the recording—as it plays. Conversely, students can highlight their notes at a certain point, and OneNote will play the corresponding recorded audio.

As with Journal, a virtual printer allows any application to print to a OneNote page. OneNote is frequently bundled with tablet PCs at purchase, and significant discounts are available to the education market.

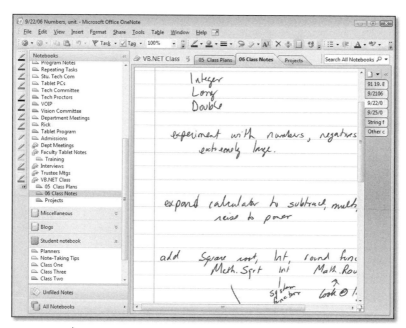

FIGURE 4.7. | OneNote users can organize their notes from directly within the application.

TABLET PCS IN THE REAL WORLD

Taking Notes: A Small Demonstration

One of our first tablet PC demonstrations was in an art history class at Vermont Academy, which offered a real-life example of what can be done with tablet PCs. Here, we used a wireless Internet connection to quickly locate an image of the picture under discussion, dropped it into Microsoft Journal, and then directly annotated the image in multiple colors to capture the content of the lecture in good detail and in real time (Fig. 4.8). This single note-taking demonstration convinced the class teacher to implement a tablet PC pilot program the following semester.

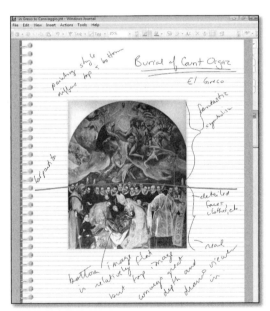

FIGURE 4.8. | This Microsoft Journal note was created on the fly during an art history class. The author cut and pasted the images from a Web page and then made notes directly onto the images as the instructor discussed the slides.

MindManager and Kidspiration

Mind-mapping programs such as Mindjet's MindManager and Inspiration Software's Inspiration and Kidspiration are important additions to this software category. Via diagrams and outlines, these applications provide impressive ways of visually representing relationships between ideas and concepts.

Inspiration and Kidspiration specifically target students in grades 6–12 and K–5, respectively. Templates, interfaces, and symbols are designed to be appropriate for the needs of students at these grade levels. The pen can be used to draw some shapes on screen and the software will convert these into symbols. Unfortunately, tablet PC integration in these packages is minimal.

MindManager is a general-use software, meaning it is not designed specifically for education. However, older students and faculty would likely find it useful. Ink is completely integrated into this system and complete mind maps can be developed with the pen and ink.

Collaboration

Although not part of personal-productivity software per se, the applications in this category provide compelling reasons to bring tablet PCs into the classroom for collaborative purposes.

Enhanced Productivity with Microsoft Office

This suite of software (typified by Word, PowerPoint, and Excel) has had some ink annotation ability for several versions, and Office 2007 features its best ink capabilities yet.

The enhancements found in Office 2007 greatly increase the usefulness of these applications on tablet PCs. Students and teachers can mark up documents and presentations on screen as easily as they can on paper versions (Fig 4.9). If a means of electronic document submission and return is used, the entire process of writing, grading, revising, and correcting papers and presentations can take place quickly and efficiently, without ever printing out a single page.

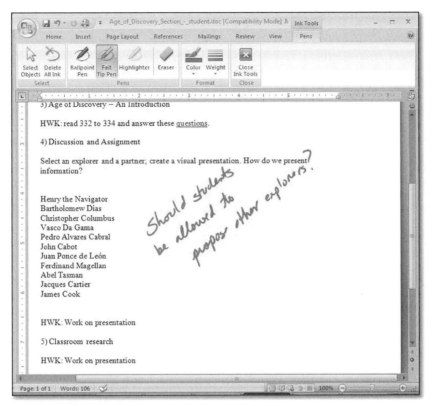

FIGURE 4.9. | Any Word document can be annotated with ink as shown here. Although earlier versions of Word (as far back as Office XP) allow for inking of documents, the Office 2007 ribbon interface makes the process quick and easy.

Enhanced Productivity via Direct Annotation

The ability to ink or to mix ink, images, and text using applications like these has many potential productivity benefits. For example, math teachers can create formulas quickly and easily with ink embedded into a Word document (rather than using a more cumbersome formula editor). Biology teachers can easily draw diagrams or annotate embedded pictures directly onto the body of a handout (rather than using a more convoluted method, or a combination of methods, to achieve a similar end). When these applications are used in conjunction with software such as DyKnow Vision, a truly collaborative educational environment can be created.

Paperless Papers

One potential productivity improvement with this type of system is that student work, when graded electronically and stored on a course management system (or when transmitted via e-mail), can be "returned" to the student as soon as it is marked or graded. This has the potential to give the student both immediate feedback and more time for work. For example, if the teacher's comments for a particular first-draft paper were normally completed on a Friday evening, the student would likely have to wait the entire weekend before seeing the comments on the next day of class; whereas a student receiving their comments electronically (by, say, Saturday morning) could have the whole weekend to work on revisions—when the work was fresher in his or her mind.

Also, although text annotations can always be done with a word-processing "track changes" feature, the tablet PC makes it possible for the teacher to grade and comment with ink—exactly the same as if he or she were working with paper drafts, including scratch-outs, symbols and margin comments.

Specialized Collaboration Software

This class of software is designed specifically to enhance the utility of tablet PCs and promote student engagement both in and out of class. DyKnow Vision, Classroom Presenter, and Ubiquitous Presenter are examples of this type of software. Though they are optimized for use with tablet PCs, they could be used in traditional 1-to-1 laptop programs or single-user situations.

In a 1-to-1 setting, teachers can present a lesson on a tablet PC or other input device, such as an electronic whiteboard. All of the information that is sketched, typed, or imported by the teacher appears immediately on each student's display. Each student can use his or her computer to make private annotations to the teacher's material, which, in turn, can be presented back to the entire class and saved for review—in many dynamic and interesting ways.

For an overview of collaborative software for the tablet PC, see "Collaboration Software" at the end of chapter 1. For a detailed look at this class of software in action, see "Cross-Discipline Classroom Interaction Tools" in the "1-to-1 Learning" section, chapter 6.

Save and Share

Although tablet PCs allow for direct annotation on course materials, the original copy of a given document can be preserved intact. Teachers do not need to make multiple physical copies of their course materials in order to use them in different classes. At the same time, teachers can preserve their annotations made in class for subsequent class reviews, for posting on a course Web site, or for modifying course materials later. PowerPoint is one application where direct annotation is beneficial. Figure 4.10 shows ink that was placed directly on a PowerPoint slide during a slide show. The ink can either be discarded or saved with the slide for later viewing.

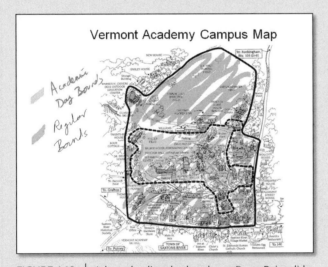

FIGURE 4.10. | Ink can be directly placed on a PowerPoint slide.

Electronic Library: Adobe Acrobat and Related Tools

As a result of their ubiquity across the globe, Adobe Portable Document Format (PDF) files have become the *lingua franca* of document exchange in the digital world. PDFs are small in size and accurately reproduce page layouts across all platforms, and Adobe Acrobat *Reader* is free. Owing to these benefits, documentation and texts of all kinds are readily available as PDF files.

Indeed, supplemental textbook materials and textbooks themselves are available as PDF files. As the textbook publishing industry moves in this direction, it is increasingly feasible to have all of one's textbooks available in this format. In addition, many Web sites provide free Acrobat versions of public domain works.

Acrobat files are excellent for use on tablet PCs, and a vast amount of them can be stored for always-ready references. And, with the keyboard folded out of the way, the act of reading PDF documents on a tablet PC is a natural activity. In effect, the tablet PC can become a portable library.

Adobe Digital School Collection

This suite of software is designed to help educators encourage student creativity through the use of multimedia software. In addition to specialized versions of Adobe programs such as Photoshop, Premiere Pro, and Acrobat, this collection includes lesson plans and tutorials. The Adobe Digital School Collection is available through flexible volume licensing options for K–12 schools and districts only (www.adobe.com/education/k12/adsc/).

Tablet PCs and PDF files fit well together in many ways and provide several subtle and not-so-subtle productivity improvements. For example, existing third-party software allows for easy creation of PDF files from other file formats. Several free PDF "printers" are also available that allow users to create a PDF file from any application that can print. PrimoPDF and CutePDF are two freeware examples of this. Office 2007 has a free add-in available for download that lets users create PDF files from Word, Excel, or PowerPoint.

Additionally, PDF Annotator from Grahl Software allows users to directly ink on any PDF file (Fig. 4.11). Software such as this allows the reader to mark and highlight content just as if reading a paper text. I have saved many days in the negotiation of a contract by annotating, editing, and signing the final copy as a PDF file on my tablet PC.

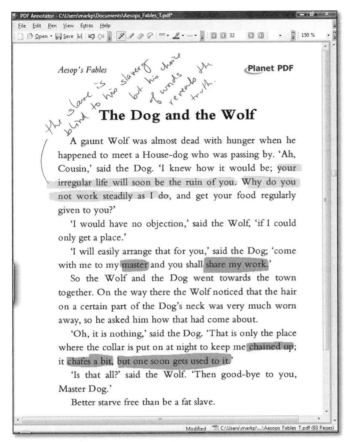

Electronic Library: MS Reader and Related Tools

Microsoft Reader is another software solution that allows users to gather a large
library of documents on the tablet PC. MS Reader should come pre-installed on
a Windows-based tablet PC. If not, it can be downloaded for free. The majority
of the books in my electronic library are in this format. Beyond an educational
setting, I use this software and my tablet PC to redeem otherwise wasted time in
doctor's offices, airports, and so forth.

Student Journalism in the 21st Century

One intriguing development in this area comes from the Missouri School of Journalism. Although this is not an example of K–12 publishing, it can nonetheless light the way for student journalism at all grade levels.

This institution publishes a weekly version of their newspaper in an electronic edition called *eMprint* (Fig. 4.12). Although it is published as a PDF document, it opens full screen and is navigable entirely with the pen. When read on a tablet PC, it provides for a rich experience.

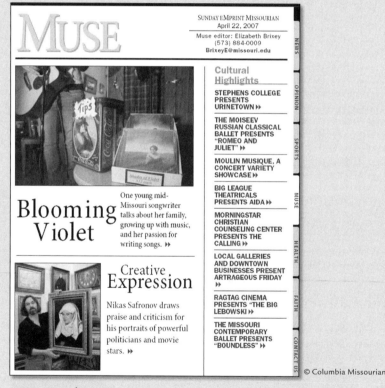

FIGURE 4.12. | Missouri School of Journalism's electronic edition of their weekly newspaper captures the feel of reading a regular newspaper in a format that works extremely well on tablet PCs.

Whereas Adobe Acrobat looks at documents as a fixed layout that must be kept consistent across platforms and screen sizes, MS Reader views documents as text that needs to be naturally readable across different screen sizes. When the screen size or orientation changes, MS Reader will reflow the text to keep line length and page size adjusted for optimal readability.

On a tablet PC, MS Reader also allows for annotation of the text with the pen, making it a feasible tool for reading class texts (Fig. 4.13). When text reflows because of a screen orientation or window size change, the ink remains associated with the text, though not always exactly as desired.

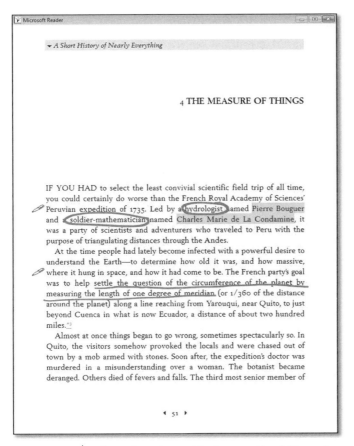

FIGURE 4.13. | Microsoft Reader provides for a good book-like reading experience, and text can be annotated with a pen.

In addition, Microsoft has a free add-in for Microsoft Word XP and 2003 that exports any Word document into an MS Reader file. A version was promised for Word 2007, but as of this writing it is not currently available.

Since minimal formatting is needed to create MS Reader documents, a large body of work in this format is available online. Project Gutenberg, for example, has a large library of public domain works available online in the MS Reader format. Many more titles in this format can be purchased online via retail sites such as Amazon.com and Barnesandnoble.com.

Other Electronic Texts

Adaptive Book is a new textbook system currently under development at Carnegie Mellon University. When completed, it promises to allow users not only to read and annotate textbooks, but to create texts from personally created or downloaded content. This same functionality also pledges to let users edit text such that, as a course develops and changes over time, an associated textbook can be modified accordingly.

Instant Messaging

You may wonder why instant messaging (IM) programs are included in a chapter on productivity. Indeed, the vast majority of instant messaging use that I have seen in schools (and elsewhere) qualifies more as productivity reduction rather than productivity enhancement. Regardless, IM is a relevant technology in the lives of our students. The question is not how to squelch its use, but how to harness it in a positive, productive manner. Indeed, IM can enhance collaboration in an educational setting, whether those collaborators are teachers or students.

In terms of the tablet PC, two IM systems stand out: Windows Messenger and Trillian Astra (currently in alpha testing as of this writing). Both support ink within messages. This feature allows for not just text to be sent in real time but also drawings and sketches.

Art Education: Unleashing the Pen

For those who like to draw, paint, or engage in digital-image manipulation, there are some excellent programs available for free that can unleash that creative bent.

ArtRage

ArtRage, from Ambient Design, is a painting program that provides a blank canvas and basic artist tools (paint brush and oils, palette knife, drawing pencil, charcoal, etc.). This software does not provide tools for making perfect circles or for touching up existing digital images; rather, it effectively mimics a real session at an easel or drawing pad. Ambient Design has some wonderful end-user-created samples at their Web site. In addition to the free version, there is an inexpensive commercial version that makes several additional tools available.

FIGURE 4.14. | Unlike many computer graphics tools that feature great power and great complexity, ArtRage provides a simple blank canvas and a set of brushes, pens, and other tools that allow for complete freedom of expression.

Paint.NET

Another free program is Paint.NET, a feature-rich image-editing and photo-manipulation tool. It supports layers, unlimited undo, and numerous special effects, such as blurring, sharpening, and red-eye removal. It also supports curve, gradient, and shape tools.

Microsoft PowerToys (Windows XP)

PowerToys is a free, downloadable group of programs for Windows XP. Among the many versions, there is one group written specifically for the tablet PC. These programs range from the purely diverting to the incredibly useful. Examples of the latter include Physics Illustrator, a motion simulator; and Writing Practice Tool, a program that encourages young students to practice writing words in freehand.

> For a more detailed description of using tablet PC PowerToys in a 1-to-1 classroom setting, see "Classroom Uses of Content-Specific Applications" in the 1-to-1 Learning section, chapter 6.

Rest and Relaxation, Tablet PC Style

One often overlooked key to maintaining productivity is taking time off for relaxation. Without down time, productivity and efficiency levels drop and the ability to concentrate is compromised.

Although relaxing for some may mean getting away from the computer altogether, games on the tablet PC can provide their own form of R&R for others. Depending on the circumstances, an electronic library might be adequate. However, if something a bit more interactive is in order, there are many free options available for the tablet PC besides solitaire.

The Microsoft Crossword Puzzle (a PowerToy) allows users to use the pen to complete a free daily crossword puzzle. In addition to that puzzle, other puzzles can be purchased for use in the program. Other PowerToys provide mazes, pool, and other games. Microsoft's Education Pack for tablet PCs includes a game called Hexic Deluxe, a pen-optimized version of the online game of the same name.

As part of their tablet PC developer support, Microsoft has released a Sudoku tablet game that includes the source code of the application (Fig. 4.15). Since this game generates the Sudoku puzzles, there is an all but unlimited supply of Sudoku puzzles for all skill levels.

FIGURE 4.15. | Among the increasing number of games designed for the tablet PC is Microsoft's Sudoku.

Course Content Management Systems

The tablet PC, with its anytime, anywhere usability, seems to be a perfect vehicle for taking advantage of digital course content management systems. In reality, it is an area full of promise for improved productivity and simultaneously a source of frustration.

Systems such as Blackboard, WebCT, Moodle, and Sakai offer tremendous potential for improving student and faculty productivity. Faculty simply post an entire set of course information online (syllabus, lessons, assignments, supporting and reference documents, etc.) and refer students, parents, or tutors to it. These users then login to get their assignments and turn them in. Faculty can retrieve those completed assignments, grade them, and return them with a heretofore unheard of efficiency. Such is the promise for enhanced class-related productivity.

Web-based applications in general are designed primarily for keyboard and mouse input. As such, they are not pen-friendly. These applications are certainly no more difficult to use on a keyboard-ready tablet PC than on a notebook computer, but they are no better either.

There are upsides to using a tablet PC with these applications. Programs such as OneNote can save documents in such a way that they are easily viewed from a Web page, even if end-users do not possess OneNote (Fig. 4.16). This allows ink-based content, such as complex math problems, to be readily accessible. In a similar way, programs such as ArtRage can export their documents in standard image formats. Other programs, such as Windows Journal and Adobe Acrobat, have free viewers that end users can download.

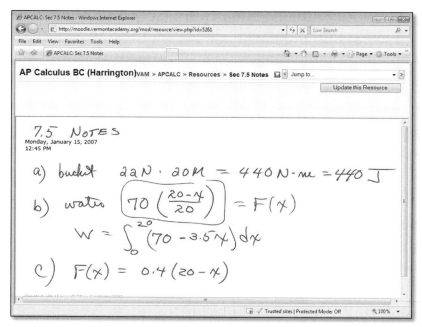

FIGURE 4.16. | OneNote documents may be exported in formats that can be posted to course content management systems.

Of course, tablet PC application files can be posted and retrieved like any other computer document. In a 1-to-1 tablet PC learning environment, the enhanced productivity benefits are readily apparent. For example, a quiz can be posted as a PDF file. Users can download the quiz and complete it using ink (including diagrams or the work required to solve a math problem). Once complete, students then submit their quiz back to the management system. There are no papers or file folders to keep track of, no chance of having too few copies of the quiz, and students don't even have to be in the same room as the teacher.

Although uploading and managing files are still manual processes, course content management systems are improving. Of particular note for tablet PC users is Blackboard Backpack from Agilix. Backpack essentially combines all the features of GoBinder (unsurprising since Agilix also wrote GoBinder), including inking ability on tablet PCs, with a behind-the-scenes management of downloading course content (Fig. 4.17). Students can keep local copies of the course content on their computers, thus making them truly available anywhere, anytime. This feature alone greatly boosts productivity potential for students.

FIGURE 4.17. | The content displayed in the Blackboard Backpack screen was automatically downloaded from the course site and now resides locally on the computer.

GoCourse Learning System

At the time of this writing, Agilix is in the process of developing a next generation course content management system, which they are calling the GoCourse Learning System (GLS). Unlike systems such as Blackboard or Moodle, which are Web applications, GLS utilizes local client applications combined with a server component. The result promises to be significantly enhanced functionality with a rich client experience—one that takes good advantage of the tablet PC's digital ink and addresses the shortcomings of Web-based systems.

The student's client promises all the features of GoBinder and Backpack, but fully automates the downloading of course materials, assignments, calendar items, and the like. In addition, completed assignments are automatically uploaded to the server without manual user intervention. Graded assignments are brought back down as instructors return them to the server.

The instructor's component allows for development of course content largely within the tool itself, locally on the instructor's tablet PC. In the same way that the student's client automates the synchronizing of content with the server, the instructor component automatically places finished content on the server for student retrieval. Assignments completed by students are downloaded behind the scenes, then returned to the server after grading. Grading tools are incorporated in the program to both assist with grading and automate the calculation and recording of grades.

The first version of GoCourse was expected to be available for use in the classroom by the end of 2007.

Challenges and Future Directions

The tablet PC is already a powerful personal productivity tool. However, there are still improvements needed for tablet PC software and hardware in order to boost personal productivity even further.

Limitations in the software written for the tablet PC can hinder personal productivity. Even five years after the introduction of the tablet PC, ink-integration problems in the operating system remain. Likewise (as of this writing), there is little support for pen input with Web browsers other than Internet Explorer (although some work has been done on a Firefox add-in to support the pen).

Web pages, particularly Web 2.0 applications, can be quite difficult to use with a pen. (Microsoft's new Web application development platform, Silverlight, promises help in this area.) Even Agilix, which early on developed pen-centric applications for tablet PCs, has backed off somewhat from its development of Backpack and GoCourse, delaying complete pen support in GoCourse for later generations.

As long as software developers do not fully embrace the pen as equal to the keyboard and mouse in an application's interface, these challenges will remain.

The hardware challenges of the tablet PC, in terms of improving personal productivity, are generally the same as those of all ultra-portable computers. Hardware vendors are scrambling to meet these challenges because many of them have cross-platform utility. These challenges include:

- **Battery life.** Batteries are improving, but, to date, no single battery can last an entire day without recharging. Likewise, batteries need to maintain their recharge longevity for several years. The current tradeoff is that more powerful batteries weigh more and are generally larger.

- **Weight.** Lighter will always be better when it comes to tablet PCs. Weights are dropping, but most tablet PCs are still over three pounds. Ideal weight is currently in direct proportional conflict with screen size and the presence of extra ports and optical drives.

- **Size.** Tablets with large external dimensions tend to be awkward and therefore less likely to be carried and available for use. Personal preference will dictate what is too big or too small; but in general, a smaller size means a smaller screen and less weight.

- **Screen size.** A U.S. standard 8.5 x 11-inch sheet of paper has a diagonal size of just under 14 inches. A4-size paper is slightly larger still. By comparison, most tablet PC screens have a diagonal screen size of 12.1 inches; meaning that, for some writers, some tablet screens may feel somewhat cramped. Generally, there is a direct correlation between screen size and the computer's external dimensions, though some manufacturers minimize this well by reducing the width of the bezel surrounding the screen.

- **Indoor/outdoor screens.** Since these screens are not usually standard on tablet PCs, they add to the cost of the systems. Nevertheless, in education, indoor/outdoor screens are extremely useful and add tremendous flexibility. With some indoor/outdoor screens, the screen clarity might be compromised, but the biggest concern may be the cost.

- **Durability**. Much like with all things carried, it is inevitable that some tablet PCs will be dropped. And some, unfortunately, will be dropped often. Many systems have added features to address this issue, such as a sensor on the hard drive that identifies rapid acceleration and parks the hard drive head. Nevertheless, screens and cases can break, keyboard hinges can crack, and keys can pop off. Ruggedized tablet PCs are available, but at a significantly higher cost. The size and weight of these models can also be a factor.

- **Instant-on performance.** "Anywhere, anytime" computing can actually translate to "anywhere, right after this thing wakes up from its sleep mode." A true instant-on capability would enhance usefulness and productivity immensely. This can be achieved fairly well with current technology, but at a great cost to battery life (since, with an instant-on option, the computer cannot be completely put to sleep). New technologies are coming to address this, but cost will likely be the initial tradeoff.

- **Video performance.** Though most tablet PCs have decent video performance under Windows XP, Vista changes the equation since it requires significantly boosted video performance. Systems that look sluggish feel sluggish, whether they really are or not. On my own Vista system, I found the Sidebar to be a real productivity boost. Nevertheless, it slowed my system down so much in other ways that I eventually turned it off. Increased video performance is the key culprit—faster video means higher costs and more heat.

- **General performance.** Many factors contribute to the overall performance of computers, and many of them have been improving steadily. Multi-core processors, dedicated video RAM and processors, higher RPM hard drives, solid state hard drives, faster system busses, optimized hardware drivers, and many other factors can boost the total performance of a given computer. But to gain that performance, users will often pay in the areas of size, heat generation, and cost.

- **Heat.** Heat management is one of the largest problems facing users of ultra-portable computers, tablet PCs included. Faster systems run hotter, and hotter systems run noisier, owing to the need for the fan(s) to run. Systems can get too hot to comfortably hold in your arm, which can become a serious concern when, for example, you're trying to write in your calendar while on the go. To make systems run cooler, however, you might need to compromise performance.

TABLET PCS IN THE REAL WORLD

Vermont Academy

The Personal Productivity of Students

There is little specific research on the productivity aspects of tablet PC use in education. A study was completed at Vermont Academy (a small, rural independent boarding and day school) in 2006 to determine precisely if tablet PC use had a demonstrable effect on the note-taking and organizational practices of high school students (Payton, 2006). This study was published in the monograph released after the "2006 Workshop on the Impact of Pen Technology in Education" (WIPTE) at Purdue University. The author of this chapter is also the author of that study.

At the time of the study, tablet PC use at Vermont Academy was voluntary, and students who used tablet PCs had purchased their own. All students who had purchased tablet PCs received a standard software package that included Agilix GoBinder. Some students had received training in the use of GoBinder, but the majority had not. Students who did not have tablet PCs generally used a paper-assignment tracking book and various three-ring binders for note taking. Most students who had tablet PCs had used these paper systems, a standard practice at the school, prior to the purchase of their tablet computer, though a number of students were new to the school and had not. Some, but not all, students had received specific training on the use of these paper systems.

Many students had problems using the paper systems at Vermont Academy. Students often forgot their assignment book or binders when going to class, and did not always remember to use this paper system to record assignments, appointments, and notes. Furthermore, they sometimes failed to keep their notes organized in appropriate binders. Often notes would be taken on random sheets of paper, which then might or might not ever get properly filed.

Students using the tablet PC had a very different experience. Students in the study replied to a survey that asked them about their tablet PC use. Specifically, the survey inquired about the various individual components of GoBinder: the task manager (used to track assignments), the calendar, and the notes section. A majority of the students who used one of these GoBinder features indicated that GoBinder was more beneficial to them than the paper system they had previously been used to.

Here are some particularly notable items in the study:

- Approximately 75% of students indicated that, in class, they were more likely to have GoBinder than a paper scheduler or notebook.

- Almost 80% indicated that the GoBinder calendar helped them to meet obligations and be better organized.

- A majority of respondents indicated that they felt their notes were better in GoBinder than on paper, though a small number felt just the opposite.

- A majority indicated that their notes were also more organized with electronic tools.

- Most students indicated that the tools in GoBinder helped them to incorporate more color-coding into their notes.

- Most respondents found the note-searching capabilities beneficial when studying.

Overall, students in the study found that when it came to their studies, the tablet PC and GoBinder were noticeably beneficial to their personal productivity.

TABLET PCS IN THE REAL WORLD

Colorado School for the Deaf and the Blind

Using Technology to Improve Student Learning and Build a Professional Learning Community

The Colorado School for the Deaf and the Blind is a state-funded school located in Colorado Springs, Colorado. The school provides comprehensive educational services for students who have visual and/or hearing impairment, from birth to age 21.

In an effort to meet all of the needs of their students, educators used digital photography and tablet PCs to both aid in student learning and to better understand the learning process of their students. Educators used this technology to modify their instruction to the point where they became effective facilitators and coaches in their students' learning. Students, in turn, became active learners—an effective approach to learning for individuals who, in addition to the usual challenges of classroom learning, also face the challenges of sight and hearing impairment.

Using digital photography and video, educators documented student progress in a more visual way than before. For example, teachers used video clips of deaf students signing their vocabulary words. Students studied the vocabulary words, decided how to sign them (many higher-level science terms do not have a one-to-one sign correlation), took video of one another signing them, downloaded them into PowerPoint, and created vocabulary presentations. This technology brought difficult and abstract concepts for deaf students to life. For visually impaired students, LCD technology allowed them to see Excel spreadsheets at an enlarged size. This larger size allowed them to access information more readily than using traditional methods of reading. An additional aid to these students was the use of audio within a PowerPoint presentation. Providing a presentation with both visual and auditory aspects met the needs of both the low vision and blind students.

Teachers reviewed student portfolio items (reflected in journals and teachers' logs) and created daily self-assessments. Teachers wrote reflections about how to improve lesson plans, collaborated to create new ideas, and developed units of instruction that provided opportunities to use technology in the teaching and learning process. This helped to ensure that the NETS became a valuable part of their teaching process. Educators applied their newly-acquired skills to improve the overall quality of their teaching.

Through this assessment process, educators noticed a tremendous impact that technology had on student learning, as well as on their own instruction techniques. They were finding, for example, that students were more easily engaged in the learning process, and that educators themselves were improving their own teaching techniques. As a result, students showed improvements not only in the use of technology but also in their knowledge, as measured by their state standards and also the NETS. Students at the Colorado School for the Deaf and the Blind seemed more confident and motivated to step up and show teachers and their classmates what they learned. The energy within the classrooms went beyond what educators thought possible.

At the outset of their technology program, educators administered pre-assessments to their students. During the course of the year, students participated in ongoing post-assessments. Using a series of collaboratively developed rubrics, educators measured students' progress. The rubrics enabled educators to better analyze student work and make meaningful classroom observations. These rubrics also allowed educators to reflect on their own teaching practices and helped them to improve their instruction.

Indeed, measuring the technology's impact on student learning was one of their top priorities. Both their mid-point and year-end data determined that students can learn, interact, and perform better in a technology-rich environment. The data that the project has generated has given a strong indication of where students are proficient and where there are areas that still need attention.

The use of this technology allowed teachers to better collaborate with one another and recognize this collaboration's importance, which was a refreshing aspect to the participants in this project. This also enabled them to be better prepared to meet the needs of their students.

The teachers wrote several articles in their school newsletters and received positive exposure on their locally televised news programs. They also began training some of their co-workers in the use of this technology, and how to incorporate it into their teaching. As a result, they gained a new energy for tackling complex issues and for facing the day-to-day grind that teaching can sometimes become.

Tomorrow is Today

The future of tablet PCs as personal productivity tools is promising on a number of fronts.

Microsoft's Vista operating system represents a significant, positive step in the evolution of tablet PCs. This software makes significant improvements for tablet PC usability, even for applications that weren't specifically designed with a digital pen in mind.

Increasingly, textbook publishers are making their texts available in electronic format—a sure boon for students and teachers using tablet PCs. Innovative developments in electronic publishing, such as the eMprint electronic newspaper from the Missouri School of Journalism, demonstrate just how tablet PCs can become a viable alternative to printed newspapers and magazines. Software tools such as Adaptive Book promise to give both students and teachers significant utility and flexibility in terms of developing and customizing texts.

Improvements in course management systems, such as Blackboard Backpack and Agilix GoCourse, should help ease both the creation and the consumption of course content. They also offer promise for facilitating the migration to an all-electronic management system of materials, assignments, and grading.

Lastly, the slow but steady improvements in the tablet PC hardware itself will serve to bring down costs, increase performance, and make tablet computing a readily available and useful tool for maximizing personal productivity for everyone in education.

5 | Bringing Single-User Settings to Life

TRACY HAMMOND
Assistant Professor, Department of Computer Science
Texas A&M University

KENRICK MOCK
Associate Professor, Department of Mathematical Sciences
University of Alaska, Anchorage

IN THIS CHAPTER

- More than a slide show: The tablet PC as a class-presentation tool

- Planning to teach with the tablet PC

- Case Studies: Ferryway School; St. Martin's Episcopal School; Goldenview Middle School

- Examples of curriculum-specific software and their uses

- Technical and human challenges of tablet PC-based instruction in a single-user setting

This chapter introduces ways that educators can use tablet PCs in single-user classroom settings. In this context, "single-user" means that students or faculty use the tablet PC in a stand-alone manner and not as a central device for communication and collaboration.

But this chapter does more than illustrate how educators can use the tablet PC for classroom presentations. It also highlights areas to consider when preparing to teach with a tablet PC, and it describes a variety of powerful software packages that, when used with a tablet PC, bring a single-user setting to life.

Presenting the Tablet PC

In the classroom, what advantages does a lone tablet PC have over more traditional technologies? Quick answers to this question, and more, are here. This section also covers the most common uses of the tablet PC in a single-user environment and alternatives to a stand-alone tablet PC in a single-user setting.

More Than a Slide Show

Perhaps the most common use of a tablet PC in the single-user classroom is as a replacement for the chalkboard or whiteboard. The process is straightforward: The instructor connects a tablet PC to a digital projector, and using software products such as Microsoft OneNote, PowerPoint, or Journal, the instructor presents a lesson while writing on the tablet PC (Fig. 5.1). The projector shows the class what is happening on the tablet PC screen.

On the surface, this presentation method is no different than one that uses a traditional overhead projector, or even one that shows PowerPoint slides from a PC. However, the tablet PC can do more than merely provide images on a blank slate or present prepared slides. Like any PC today, the tablet PC can run complex software, as well as store and display vast amounts of useful data. And, of course, it can connect wirelessly to the Internet. But here's a significant difference: What would otherwise be a static presentation (even if those PowerPoint slides have animations, videos, and Web pages) becomes a dynamic experience, complete with hand-written notes and voice commentary that can be recorded, saved, and posted online for students to review from any PC.

A math teacher can show a function changing over time; a Japanese language teacher can demonstrate the sequence of strokes to draw a character; finally, a student can go home after school, go online, and review both lessons.

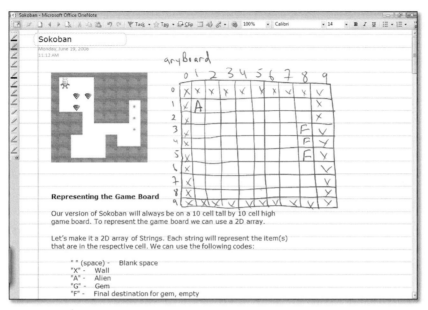

FIGURE 5.1. │ Using OneNote, an instructor created a slide prior to class. The hand-drawn grid was created on the fly during the presentation.

Better, Cleaner Presentations

Tablet PC-based instruction has numerous other advantages over traditional presentations on a chalkboard or via an overhead projector; for example:

- The instructor can easily re-visit and display previously covered material that would have otherwise been erased.

- The instructor has convenient access to digital pens and highlighters (in many different colors and sizes).

- The instructor can easily switch to other computer applications, such as a Web browser.

- The instructor never has to deal with messy chalk, marker ink, or dry erasers.

- The instructor never blocks the view of the projector (unlike when blocking the chalkboard while writing). Indeed, the instructor can move about the class while writing. Freed from the stage, a teacher never again has to turn his or her back to write on a chalkboard.

Interactive Whiteboards: A Big Alternative

In single-user technology situations, there are alternatives to the tablet PC itself. Interactive whiteboards, as the name implies, are large-surface display devices designed for presenting information to a group or class. Simply, the instructor projects a PC's computer display (most any PC will do) to a large pen-input display. For instructors who already have a PC in the classroom, or who require (or prefer) a large display surface, using an interactive whiteboard is a viable alternative to using a tablet PC and a projector.

> For an overview of interactive whiteboards and other tablet PC alternatives with their many benefits, see "Larger Displays" (p. 22) in chapter 1.

However, an interactive whiteboard works best in combination with a tablet PC. The instructor simply connects his or her tablet PC to an interactive whiteboard (either directly or via a projector), then writes on either surface. When a large writing surface is needed, the instructor can write on the whiteboard. When mobility or flexibility matters most, the instructor can make notes on his or her tablet PC.

> Pen-based collaboration software is a natural addition to a classroom with both an interactive whiteboard and a tablet PC. For using this software in the classroom, see the "1-to-1 Learning" section, chapter 6.

TABLET PCS IN THE REAL WORLD

Ferryway School

Using 21st-Century Technology to Study the Technological Needs of Colonists in the New World

Ferryway School is a K–8 math, science, and technology-magnet school in Malden, Massachusetts. Although Ferryway School emphasizes the skills and processes of all academic areas, its focus is on the integration of mathematics, science, and computer skills that enable students to comprehend the world of scientific inquiry.

This case study focuses on how an HP Technology for Teaching Grant enabled Ferryway School's Saugus Iron Works Project-Based Unit (PBU) to move into the 21st century.

Saugus Iron Works, a National Historic Site, is located just outside of Boston in Saugus, Massachusetts. It is the site of North America's first integrated ironworks, in operation from 1646 to 1668. Ferryway School students were tasked to learn about the uses of technology at this colonial ironworks, among other things.

Areas of study in this PBU included a mineral profile lesson and a postcard lesson. In the past, students drew pictures of minerals and colonial times using traditional classroom materials such as pen and paper. But with the introduction of the HP equipment, the continuous use of the tablet PC, projector, and camera, teachers enhanced student learning and their own teaching strategies.

The mineral profile lesson was done using the tablet PC and a digital camera. Students took pictures of the minerals and uploaded them to the computer. The colonial times lesson was also changed. Students took pictures of objects during a field trip to Saugus Iron Works and then uploaded these photos to create postcards with realistic images.

On the surface, these may seem like small changes but they had huge implications. Since educators used more technology in the classroom (projectors, tablet PCs, cameras in place of overheads and worksheets), they were able to establish a school-wide technological framework.

Using a program called Inspiration, educators integrated the teaching of writing, science, English and language arts, social studies, computer science, and technology. Students used Inspiration to create graphic organizers as a way of brainstorming prior to writing. For example, they created organizers on the various types of rocks as a pre-writing assignment prior to creating their mineral profiles.

Likewise, educators used technology to extend learning. Using a multimedia program called Breeze, teachers enhanced student understanding and engagement with course content. Educators developed a Breeze presentation to teach the design and building process of a working waterwheel. Educators then developed a survey in Breeze to assess student learning after they observed and interacted with the waterwheel presentation.

The classroom experience has also changed at Ferryway School. Since teachers now frequently use technology to engage students in daily lessons, Ferryway has moved away from teacher-directed lessons and moved toward more student-centered collaborative activities. As teachers became facilitators of learning, students became active learners who worked in collaborative groups that navigated through lessons like the Saugus Iron Works PBU. The tablet PC in particular was instrumental in this change. Using tablet PCs, teachers were able to freely move around the classroom, which allowed for better monitoring of the students. The tablet PC's inking feature, used in conjunction with software programs and the projector, lent itself to quick, easy, and visually-appealing lessons.

Educators reflected on teaching strategies and growth throughout the HP teaching grant process. They felt that their increased knowledge of how to operate and implement computers in the classroom was extremely beneficial for them and their students. The camera allowed educators to enhance teaching, improve classroom discussion, document students' progress, and "capture the moments." For example, students were able to visually analyze their waterwheel design prototypes and make improvements during the redesign process.

In addition, peer observation allowed educators to observe and support one another, as well as build self-confidence in their own technology skills. It also allowed them to collaborate and work to improve their teaching strategies, especially in the area of technology. The self-assessments allowed them the opportunity to see their growth from beginning to end.

The impact on student learning using technology was easily observable. At the beginning of the HP grant, educators gave the students a pre-assessment to determine their background knowledge in technology and in the various content areas. The students were assessed again midway through the project, and a final assessment was also administered. The findings showed a significant increase in the number of students who actually did homework using the computer—up from 64% to 78%. Students used school-sponsored blog sites and the PBU site to do homework and research. The students also exhibited greater enthusiasm, longer retention, and more in-depth knowledge of the subject matter. The students not only improved their skills for working cooperatively, but they were also proud to share their work with peers and teachers alike.

The benefits extended beyond the classroom into the community. The new equipment allowed educators to communicate with their students' parents and the wider school community. Information pages for parents have since been adapted and translated into Chinese, with plans to include Spanish, Vietnamese, and Portuguese, translations. Moreover, this technology integration process helped to develop leadership qualities in all of the team members. Administrators provided district-wide professional development using the work and research created at Ferryway School. The work was of such quality that the Superintendent of Malden Public Schools took this project-based unit and presented it in China.

For all its success beyond the classroom, however, the Saugus Iron Works PBU was still focused on the students. Perhaps Teacher Learning Center director Robert Simpson said it best: "I had the opportunity to accompany students on the Saugus Iron Works field trip recently. Students engaged park rangers with in-depth discussions of why colonists needed technology in the New World. It should be noted that this addresses the unit's essential question."

Prep Time: Planning to Teach with a Tablet PC

Teachers who want to incorporate a stand-alone tablet PC into their classroom have some adjustments to make. These adjustments range from lesson development and getting comfortable with the technology to student learning and assessment.

Adapting to Tablet Technology

For instructors who are already computer-literate, the tablet PC learning curve is short. Learning to connect a projector to the tablet PC should be simple enough. And although getting comfortable with the tablet PC's software and pen functionality takes some diligence and practice, it is not exceedingly difficult.

Delivering a presentation with a tablet PC requires a bit more skill, in that the instructor must decide how to use the many new tools (such as highlighters) that may not have been available in a chalkboard environment. Again, mastery is a matter of practice. Many instructors who already highlight or emphasize content with "attention marks"—check marks, circles, underlines, and dashes—will find themselves right at home using a tablet PC.

Privacy Matters

We recommend that instructors close all private applications—such as e-mail—on their tablet PCs before connecting to the classroom projector. Doing so will avoid the unintentional display of private content, should unwanted programs inadvertently toggle or become maximized in full screen mode.

More significant is the time required to adapt instructional material to the medium of the tablet PC. For many teachers, this entails creating templates in software such as PowerPoint, OneNote, or Journal. No matter how simple or elaborate, these templates should feature some blank spaces. During the presentation, the instructor can write in these blank spaces to help explain the material.

Although this preparation may be time consuming, these completed templates can be used in future classes.

Intelligent Editing

Although writing on PowerPoint slides during a presentation mimics the experience of hand-written notes on a transparency or chalkboard, in truth it provides other worlds of possibilities. Many impressive software tools already exist—or are being developed—that make the migration to single-user tablet PC instruction a compelling and intelligent choice.

Single-Stroke Editing

Most tablet PC programs provide the ability to delete single strokes. This is a significant advantage over marker or chalk drawings, since the instructor can delete a single stroke even if two strokes are drawn on top of each other. What's more, drawn diagrams can be copied, deleted, or moved using lasso methods (which can be more convenient than erasing ink using the back of a tablet PC's pen).

ScanScribe

ScanScribe is an interesting tablet PC-based drawing tool that groups drawn strokes for ease of drawing. It provides intelligent editing tools that can automatically select the desired content using perceptual grouping rules. Using ScanScribe, an instructor can deliver a lesson that consists of handwriting, drawing strokes, typed-text, and images.

Drawings Brought to Life

The tablet PC can provide an intuitive way to prepare PowerPoint-enhanced lessons. However, it is difficult for a computer to understand and recognize drawn diagrams. A newly developed field called "sketch recognition" has begun to address the recognition of diagrams for use in a variety of educational subject areas. These software systems can help your drawings come alive.

> For a description of subject-specific sketch-recognition software, see "Curriculum-Specific Software and Uses" in this chapter.

Software in this category allows teachers to draw diagrams from scratch on a tablet PC, thereby stimulating student attention. Hand-drawn diagrams also promote creative visualization (hand-drawn diagrams imply the possibilities of change, development, and creation) and encourage a functional understanding of the material. Instructors can use these applications to engage students and explain material in a more interactive manner.

The Future of Sketch Recognition

Creating diagrams by finding the appropriate shape from the drop-down menus in PowerPoint can be difficult. Research is currently underway toward allowing users to sketch PowerPoint diagrams as they would naturally on a piece of paper. For example, while users sketch squares, arrows, and polygons, the software "watches" the user draw, recognizing each shape, and creates the appropriate PowerPoint shape on screen.

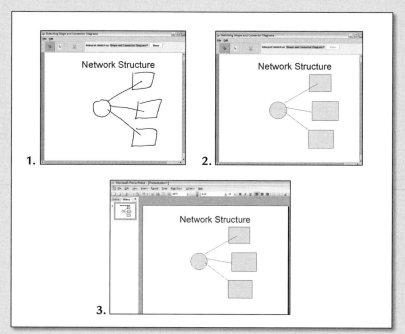

FIGURE 5.2. | A sketched diagram (1), is recognized (2), and imported into PowerPoint (3).

For the Record: Saving and Sharing Presentations

The ability to save a lesson as a document (as a Web page, an Acrobat file, a PowerPoint document, etc.) or a video presentation presents several opportunities for student learning beyond the traditional classroom.

To generate such documents and videos, many software packages exist. For single-user presentations, two popular choices include Camtasia Studio and Adobe Captivate. Several studies indicate that students overwhelmingly find class recordings valuable. There is also evidence of an increase in student academic performance, along with an increase in student attention, attendance, excitement, and understanding (Carryer, 2006; Mock, 2004). For classrooms with a 1-to-1 computing environment, we recommend a recording software that encourages collaboration.

For an overview of the software discussed in this section, see "Tablet PC Software" in chapter 1.

First, class recordings allow students to review a lesson even if they miss class. This can be easily accomplished if the instructor's class notes are made available for download. Second, these recordings allow students to review material at their own pace. In some cases, a student's pace may be slower, in which case he or she can review the lecture material multiple times; or the pace may be faster, in which case the student can skip over material already understood.

A screen-recorded video capture of the lesson is particularly effective for both scenarios, especially in combination with an audio recording of the instructor's voice. Simply put, an inked document will be less meaningful and may even be difficult to understand without the audio narrative given in class.

It should be noted that files of recorded lessons have the potential to be quite large. Depending on the frame rate of the recording, the size of the screen, the desired video quality, and the content of the recording, a one-hour presentation could require anywhere from 15 to 50 MB (or more) of storage. In most cases, the videos will be accessible to viewers with high-speed Internet connections and inaccessible to those using dial-up speeds.

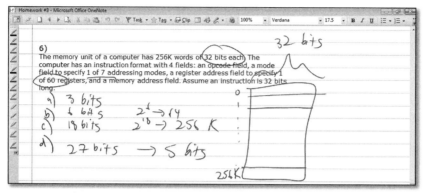

FIGURE 5.3. | This OneNote document was explained during class. However, it is somewhat vague and mysterious without an oral explanation. A video recording can remedy this problem.

Distance Learning

The tablet PC can serve as a useful accessory to distance learning environments. In its simplest form, class notes and screen-captured video can be saved and then placed online for students to access remotely. However, when used in combination with synchronous distance-education software, such as Elluminate or Adobe Connect, an ink-based presentation can be shared live with remote students over the Internet.

These software packages not only allow remote students to view the content shown on the instructor's screen (while simultaneously receiving the instructor's audio), but they also support blended classrooms, whereby an instructor can present the material in a physical classroom while simultaneously broadcasting the presentation over the Internet.

TABLET PCS IN THE REAL WORLD

St. Martin's Episcopal School
Teaching 11th- and 12th-Grade Pre-Calculus, Calculus, and Trigonometry

St. Martin's Episcopal School is a private school that serves PK–12 and is located in Metairie, Louisiana. In the fall of 2006, the school began equipping all students from the eighth grade (and higher) with tablets.

Jim Marsalis teaches 11th- and 12th-grade pre-calculus, calculus, and trigonometry classes. He uses a tablet PC in his classroom for presentation purposes and has also experimented with online video lectures. Marsalis' classroom is equipped with a tablet PC, projector, and a Mimio interactive whiteboard. However, he rarely uses the Mimio because he feels that the tablet PC can do everything the interactive whiteboard can do, but more efficiently.

Prior to lecture, Marsalis develops an outline of the lesson using Microsoft OneNote. This entails adding hyperlinks, figures, text, or ink to provide the framework for the lesson that is later expanded upon during the actual lecture. In addition to OneNote, Marsalis also incorporates a variety of mathematical software in his lectures, including Geometer's Sketchpad (for visualization of mathematical concepts), Winplot (to dynamically draw curves and surfaces), and TI Interactive (to show an on-screen calculator). Switching among these software programs is easy on the tablet PC. All that is needed is to simply select the desired program from the task bar. In a traditional classroom, an instructor would have to physically switch between the computer and the blackboard.

After the lecture, Marsalis makes the tablet-generated lecture notes available to his class.

Marsalis also uses a mathematical sketch-recognition system called FluidMath. Although still in a pre-release form, FluidMath allows the instructor to write and draw equations, diagrams, and objects by hand. Drawn equations are recognized mathematically and can then be graphed using a special gesture of the pen. Similarly, equations can be associated with objects and then animated. For example, the instructor might draw a circle to represent a ball, write the equations that govern the ball's motion, and then (with the appropriate pen gesture) move the circle as described by the equations. Marsalis currently uses the system to demonstrate mathematical concepts, and eventually the students may use the software themselves, as the sketch recognition and ease of use improve over time.

Marsalis has also begun to experiment with video lecture recordings. Using the My Screen Recorder software, he has produced WMV files of his screen. Although the WMV format is lossy (the resulting video file may be fuzzy in places and is not an exact copy of the original screen), the resulting file size is relatively small. The software also supports output in the popular Flash video format, which is not lossy.

Marsalis has experimented with recording lectures and lessons, both in-class and at home. Some of these videos were assigned as homework problems for the students to view, while others were shown in class as part of a lecture. Under this system, students can watch a video lesson and then immediately work on problems. This setup allows more one-to-one time for working on problems in class and less time spent teaching material that can be learned more effectively outside of class.

Interestingly, Marsalis prefers the made-at-home videos to those recorded during class. "I thought they needed my dramatic, charismatic form at the board, but students seem happier with just hearing my almost-droning 'video voice'," he reports. Some instructors may feel uncomfortable putting a video file online that contains errors for "the world" to see. The made-at-home videos can be better scripted and have fewer errors than the spontaneous videos recorded during class. Although it is possible to remove errors in in-class videos using video-editing software, this process can also be time consuming and is not likely to be performed by a teacher under time constraints.

A few adjustments were necessary to incorporate tablet PCs in the classroom. First, Marsalis reports that he did a lot more sitting at the tablet PC rather than standing at the board. Second, more technology means more wires and more pieces of equipment where something could go wrong, resulting in more troubleshooting work. Finally, a significant amount of work is required to prep lecture material on the tablet PC (in this case, using ink within OneNote). However, in the end this appears to result in a better-organized lesson plan and a template that can be re-used in the future.

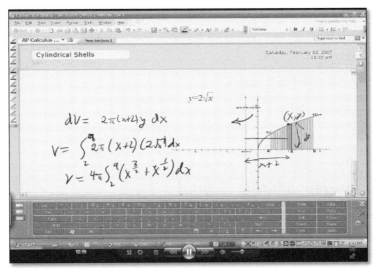

FIGURE 5.4. | Video lecture of Cylindrical Shells posted online for students. Image courtesy of Jim Marsalis, St. Martin's Episcopal School.

Marsalis reports that students have given him very positive feedback regarding the video demos. After showing a 15-minute video lecture in class, he noted that students were able to sit through it without losing attention; moreover, he received better questions from the students afterwards.

In the future, Marsalis intends to use the tablet PC in combination with the Thinkwell online textbook. Here, after watching recorded videos, the students will work out problems on their tablets and send their answers to their instructor electronically. Since the school is moving to a 1-to-1 computing environment, it will also be possible for students to use the tablets as communication devices in order to take and share notes, as well as take tests on the tablet. Technologies to support these types of 1-to-1 environments are discussed in chapter 6.

Impact on Student Learning

The tablet PC-based classroom offers several benefits with regard to presentation. But do students learn better than they would in a normal classroom? Student performance has been difficult to assess. Though this chapter is devoted to tablet PCs in a single-user setting, it should be noted that studies in 1-to-1 environments have shown an increase in student performance (Koile & Singer, 2006).

The results are mixed when a tablet is used primarily for presentation. In all cases, students were generally favorable toward the tablet PC and there was an increase in student excitement and attention.

TABLET PCS IN THE REAL WORLD

Goldenview Middle School
Teaching Eighth-grade Algebra and Pre-Algebra

Goldenview Middle School is a public middle school located in Anchorage, Alaska, that serves the seventh and eighth grades. This case study focuses on Mike Truskowski's eighth-grade algebra and pre-algebra math classes.

Truskowski's classroom consists of a single tablet PC for the instructor and a wireless data projector. The classroom was also equipped, on loan, with a Promethean Activboard and a Promethean Activote system. Activboard is an interactive whiteboard and Activote is a Personal Response System (PRS). A PRS is a "clicker" (passed out to each student) that resembles a small remote control with buttons to answer multiple-choice or true-false questions. When a question is posed on the computer and projected on the screen, each student then answers on the PRS. Statistics on how all students voted is collected on the computer and can be displayed back to the class. The data displayed to the class is anonymous, while the student's name and a record of how they voted is stored by the computer for later analysis by the teacher. As complementary technology to the tablet PC, the "clicker" encourages every student to actively participate in the exercises, and it provides feedback to the instructor regarding class comprehension—yet another means to engage students.

As with the St. Martin's School case study, Truskowski also preferred the tablet PC to the interactive whiteboard. Not only is the tablet PC more efficient, it's also faster. Truskowski reported a slight lag when using the pen on the interactive whiteboard that is not present with the tablet PC. He also was able to take the tablet computer and wireless projector adaptor to any classroom and be teaching within minutes.

The wireless projector is a key component to how Truskowski conducts his class. In his classroom the tablet PC sends its video directly to the data projector, wirelessly (via radio frequency), eliminating the need for a video cable. While this may seem like it is only a convenience to eliminate the video cable, there is a major benefit: the instructor is no longer tethered to one location by the video cable. Truskowski uses this to his advantage by taking the tablet into his class and working with (or handing it out) to students. The student working on the tablet can then share his or her work with the entire class via the wireless link to the projector. Truskowski found that students preferred this type of interaction compared to him (or them) getting up in front of the class and writing on the board.

The software centerpiece of Truskowski's tablet lectures is Microsoft Journal, which he uses to store lecture templates. Prior to class he determines what exercises, figures, images, Web sites, or other content he will use for the lesson, and then he creates a template for the lesson in Journal. For example, the template might contain exercises to be covered in class. In this case, the template would contain only the problems and not the solutions. During class, the template is loaded and serves as a lecture guide as the problems are solved using the pen. The completed Journal files from lecture are later converted to HTML and uploaded online (Fig. 5.5). Students can then view the notes after class. In addition to the lecture notes, Truskowski also posts assignments, schedules, and solutions on the Web.

Although Microsoft Journal lacks some of the features found in Microsoft OneNote, Truskowski prefers Journal to OneNote. In addition to greater simplicity and a familiar file-based organization of documents, Journal does not automatically save ink. The user must explicitly take action to save the document. In contrast, the default behavior of Microsoft OneNote is to automatically save the document every few seconds. The auto-save feature is useful for note taking, but not as desirable for an instructor who wishes, for example, to keep the original lecture template intact without having to erase all of the material that was written down during class. In contrast, an instructor can create a template in Journal, ink on it during class, and then quit the program without saving changes. This leaves the template intact for future classes and reduces prep time.

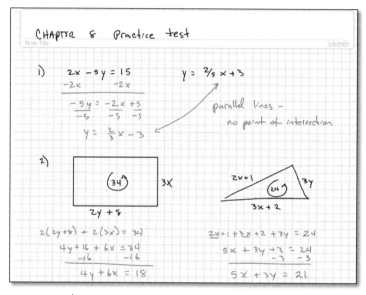

FIGURE 5.5. | Microsoft Journal file showing exercises completed in class. The document was converted to HTML and posted online. The questions are stored in a Journal file which serves as a template, while answers are completed during class.
(Image courtesy of Mike Truskowski, Goldenview Middle School)

Outside of the classroom, Truskowski also uses Journal to create his schedules, lesson plans, assignments, and solutions. Journal allows all of this content to be aggregated in one document, which also makes it an excellent communication device to give to a substitute teacher.

Truskowski reports that, after implementing tablet PCs in the classroom, he has observed better modeling on behalf of the students. As a result, the assignments turned in by students better match the format and structure expected by the instructor. Moreover, there is great excitement from the students as they see the technology in action and are able to use it themselves. Additionally, by posting the course material online, Truskowski reports that some parents have read his material and used it to help their children at home.

Finally, Truskowski has created video recordings to provide extra help for difficult topics. In the future he is interested in additional lecture recordings for helping to correct common errors he has observed over the years. He plans to continue using the personal response system, add more Internet resources to help with class work, and explore the possibilities with a 1-to-1 tablet environment for students.

Student Use: Please Pass the Tablet

In addition to serving as a useful tool for faculty, tablet PCs are also extremely useful when put in the hands of students. In a single user setting, students can use a tablet PC to take handwritten class notes. They can also use it in the role of a traditional computer (e.g., to help write a paper or conduct research on the Internet). But they can use it to do even more.

> The tablet PC can also serve as a collaboration tool between students and faculty. Collaboration and 1-to-1 applications are discussed in chapter 6.

Recording Instruction

Just as the instructor can record activity on his or her screen using software such as Camtasia Studio, students can use a tablet PC to record their instructors' audio and synchronize it with their own handwritten or typed-in notes. Note taking is discussed in more detail in chapter 4, which focuses on personal productivity.

Homework Assignments

The tablet PC's ability to seamlessly integrate digital ink with typed-in text makes it a versatile platform for students who need to complete a variety of homework assignments. For an assigned paper, students can easily incorporate hand-drawn diagrams or figures. Images can also be imported into a document and annotated by the student. If the assignment is provided electronically, students can also type or write their answers directly on the assigned document. In this way, tablet PCs are particularly useful for completing short-answer questions or for providing answers that require equations, diagrams, or pictures. And because these assignments are digital, they can easily be distributed and collected.

Flash Cards

Several software packages are available that can effectively turn the tablet PC into a giant set of flash cards. For example, the student can write, type, or insert an image for the question and answer, and the program randomly selects cards for the student to view.

Digital Books

The tablet PC makes an excellent digital book reader. Rather than lug many heavy textbooks about, students can read entire books or chapters of interest via the tablet PC.

Curriculum-Specific Software and Uses

In the same way that tablet PC users can use off-the-shelf software like OneNote and Journal to create hand-written documents for a "word-oriented" subject like language arts, they can use sketch-recognition software to enhance the study of art, music, chemistry, mathematics, and other graphic-oriented subjects.

In a nutshell, these sketch interfaces allow teachers and students to draw diagrams with either computer-trained or human-learned gestural input (with the implication that each shape is drawn in a particular style) or as they would naturally on a piece of paper (with the computer recognizing the shape by geometrical, rather than stylistic, properties).

Either way, the result is straightforward and incredibly useful. For example, hand-written mathematical equations can be automatically recognized by the computer and converted into clean, typed-out formulas.

The samples highlighted here are by no means exhaustive. Rather, they are meant to illustrate a range of applications and suggest ways that students can benefit from their use in a single-user setting. In the future, we can expect additional tablet-specific software in a variety of disciplines.

A Matter of Recognition

Recognizing and understanding hand-drawn sketches is quite difficult to program into a computer. Much research has been done toward recognizing gestures, segmenting strokes, recognizing geometric primitives, and performing higher-level recognition.

Each of these areas of research contains a number of difficulties. For example, users do not draw "perfectly" or consistent with each other, and recognition systems must be capable of handling varying amounts of "noise" in hand-drawn sketches. Researchers continue to address these problems today.

Moreover, a sketch-recognition interface can offer a number of possible uses, including:

- Providing vivid interactive examples

- Providing practice material to the student

- Providing immediate feedback to the student

- Providing feedback to the instructor about the student's difficulties with the material (possibly over a network)

- Automating the correction of hand-drawn graphical homework

- Automating the correction of in-class tests

Art

A sketch-recognition interface is ideal for creating art. CorelDraw and other popular paint programs provide excellent pressure sensitivity and drawing capabilities. Users can draw with a pen as they would on paper, but the drawing can be saved, edited, copied, shared, and modified. This software provides an excellent interface for art, as students can share drawings amongst each other and the instructor.

There is an ongoing discussion as to whether or not an instructor should edit a student's drawing. One philosophy says that the work should remain unchanged, as it is by nature the result of the student's creative work and is often considered the student's own "statement." Another philosophy says that editing a student's artistic work is an excellent way of teaching students how they can improve their technique. By using a tablet PC and saving a second copy, the instructor can both edit the student's work and leave the original creation intact.

Music

Hand-sketching music notes is a natural way for editing and composing musical notes. The Music Notepad provides pen-gesture input of musical notes.

LADDER Sheet Music allows a user to hand-sketch a staff and notes on a blank screen just as he or she would naturally on a blank sheet of paper—as opposed to the software "recognizing" learned gestures—and then plays the sketched notes. This application is downloadable from http://srl.csdl.tamu.edu/musicscribble.shtml.

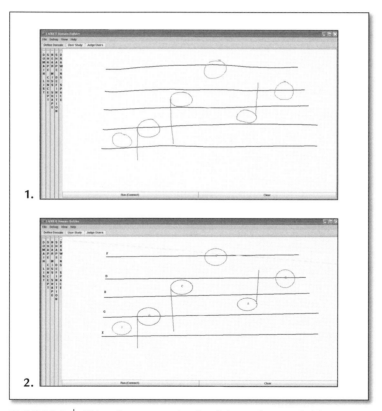

FIGURE 5.6. | This software recognizes hand-drawn sheet music (1), and then interprets and plays it (2).

Chemistry

Chemistry is a natural domain for sketch recognition. ChemPad is one such system that generates chemical diagrams from hand-drawn sketches (Fig. 5.7).

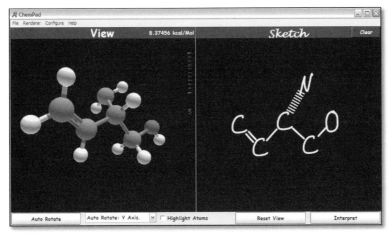

FIGURE 5.7. | ChemPad software interprets a sketched chemical diagram.

Mathematics

Given the difficulty of typing out mathematical equations, math is a natural domain for sketching by hand. But formatting mathematical equations properly can be quite difficult for users. Dedicated editors, such as the document preparation system LaTeX, have been created with the goal of simplifying mathematical formatting on the computer. xThink's MathJournal (www.xthink.com) and MathPad2 (Fig. 5.8) are two systems that rely on sketch recognition to generate corresponding mathematical formulas and graphs.

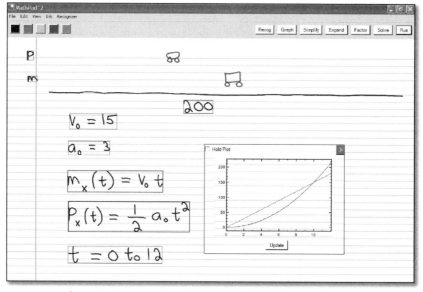

FIGURE 5.8. | MathPad2 recognizes mathematical expressions.

Challenges of Tablet PC-based Instruction

Despite the advantages of tablet PC-based instruction, there are also a number of challenges.

Technical Challenges

Although the tablet PC can store many pages of text and ink, only one page can be displayed at a time. This roughly limits the instructor to the equivalent of one blackboard "panel." This can be a detriment to presentations that require a lot of context. For example, in a traditional classroom with a large chalkboard an instructor might write some equations on one panel and then use those equations to solve a problem on a different panel. On a tablet PC, the instructor will likely have to scroll or toggle back and forth between the screen with the original equations and the one with the current problem. This obstacle can be mitigated by using digital projectors and large-display digital whiteboards. If, for whatever reason, digital projectors or whiteboards are not available, the lesson may need to be redesigned to incorporate the necessary equations. This, of course, means additional preparatory work.

Another challenge to tablet PC-based presentations is when the computer itself is tethered to the data projector via a video cable. This in turn requires the instructor to be tethered to the computer, which in turn prevents the instructor from going out into the classroom or passing the tablet PC to the students. Wireless data projectors exist, the use of which effectively solves this problem. Likewise, inexpensive "wireless" accessories can be added to existing digital projectors that effectively cut the cable. In this context, we can easily imagine classes like those of Jim Marsalis and Mike Truskowski, where the instructor presents a lesson using a tablet PC and a wireless projector.

When a student has a question but is unable to explain it verbally, instructors can simply walk over to the student and work through the problem while writing notes on the tablet PC for others in the class to see.

In some cases, however, a tether may be an advantage. Tethered instruction was used by a colleague of one of the authors who, after she broke her leg, could not easily write on the board in her usual manner. Interestingly, this instructor kept using the tablet PC for presenting lessons even after her leg had healed.

Human and Administrative Challenges

Every organization that adopts tablet technologies faces human and administrative challenges.

Adequate funding must be found to purchase the technology. Although a tablet PC is more expensive than a regular notebook computer (currently by a few hundred dollars), the added expense provides additional functionality that is profoundly rewarding. What's more, tablet PC prices continue to fall and the price gap between tablet PCs and their regular notebook counterparts is narrowing.

In addition to acquiring and maintaining the technology itself, an educational organization must provide training and technical support to both its faculty and students. Without adequate training, the technology will not be used to its potential.

For example, at one of the author's institutes, a traditional classroom was converted into a "smart" classroom. This classroom had an integrated computer with a tablet screen, digital projector, multi-disk DVD/VHS, a document camera (capable of projecting transparencies, slides, or physical objects), and a control box to select which data source to display on the screen. Despite this comprehensive technology, some faculty members brought in their own overhead projectors to show transparencies and their own TV sets on carts to show videos.

Future Directions

As tablet PC adoption grows and technologies such as multi-touch mature, we can expect new and creative uses for tablet PCs. Advancements in computer science now allow data to be directly written, digitally stored, and analyzed on the tablet PC (instead of transferring data from handwritten notes to a computer). In bench science, tablet PCs have been effectively used as electronic lab surfaces, where students perform small-scale chemistry experiments directly on the tablet and next to their handwritten structures and notes (Thompson, 2006). Even in non-technical fields such as theater, tablet PCs have been used as a staging tool for direction and choreography (Crocker, 2006).

Although tablet PCs today comprise a small segment of the market (as compared to traditional laptops), their use and growth in education and other vertical segments is strong. A study by the Greaves Group (Greaves Group, 2006) estimates that, from 2007 to 2012, there will be 78% growth in the use of tablet PCs in education, compared to 25% for PC laptops and 24% for Macs. This growth is reinforced by 24% of superintendents reporting plans to institute 1-to-1 computing initiatives in 2006, up from only 4% in 2003. Another likely growth area is the Ultra Mobile PC, which may be an attractive computing device for institutions with lower budgets. Key to the successful deployment of these technologies in education will be adequate professional development for both administrators and faculty.

As these computing initiatives gain momentum, we can expect to see tablet technologies become commonplace in the classroom. Many schools and districts have already placed fixed data projectors for use with laptops in every classroom. It may not be long before the tablet PC joins the overhead projector as another ubiquitous piece of classroom technology.

6 | Tablet PCs and 1-to-1 Learning

DAVE BERQUE
Computer Science Department
DePauw University

IN THIS CHAPTER

- Answers for why tablet PCs are superior to traditional laptops in 1-to-1 deployments

- Tablet PC hardware and software features that enhance student engagement and learning

- An illustration of collaborative software in action: DyKnow Vision in Action

- Case studies: Bishop Hartley High School; Auburn City Schools

- Impacts of 1-to-1 deployments

Can you imagine trying to teach a student to ride a bicycle merely by explaining the process? Regardless of how carefully the explanation is crafted, most of us would agree that this kind of hands-off instruction is only a recipe for disaster!

It would not matter how gifted the student is, nor how talented and experienced the teacher is. It would not even help if the teacher repeated the explanation multiple times. And requiring the student to read a textbook on bicycle riding would not solve the problem. Nor would it help if the teacher climbed on the bicycle and demonstrated how to take it for a spin. Not even a beautifully-crafted PowerPoint presentation, chock full of flashy animations, sound-effects, screen transitions, and fly-ins would bring success. As long as the teacher keeps the bicycle out of the hands (and feet) of the student, learning will be hindered.

1-to-1 Tablet PC Deployments: A Focus on Content

The bicycle example serves to illustrate a clear core concept: Most teachers would agree that an engaged student is more likely to learn than a passive student, a doer is more likely to learn than a listener, and a participant is more likely to learn than a bystander.

This chapter explores ways to foster student engagement through 1-to-1 tablet PC deployments. In the context of instructional technology, the phrase "1-to-1 computing" means just that—one computer for each student in class. The premise is simple: The interactive nature of computers can help students become engaged in course content. More importantly, when used in conjunction with appropriate software, computers can also help the teacher and students to engage each other.

But why use tablet PCs instead of traditional laptops to support a 1-to-1 deployment? The answer follows from the type of content students will interact with in many classes. This content often includes a significant amount of graphical material, including maps, graphs, charts, scribbles, and diagrams. Examples from a variety of subject areas include:

- Shapes and sketches in an art class

- Editing marks in a writing class

- Inclined planes in a physics class

- Map annotations in a history class

- Molecules in a chemistry class

- Equations and graphs in a mathematics class

- Musical notations in a music class

- Supply–demand curves in an economics class

- Kanji characters in a Japanese language class

Using only a mouse and keyboard to work with this type of content can be a tedious process. Indeed, it requires the student to focus intently on the *process of creating* the content. Unfortunately, this focus on process often comes at the expense of critically thinking about the *material itself* and its *significance* to the topic being taught.

Worse, dialog between students can easily digress into immaterial discussions about the technology alone: "No, John, you need to hold down *control* and *shift* and then press the *plus-sign* to get a superscript." Tablet PCs provide a more natural input mechanism for many types of content, thereby freeing the students to become engaged in the material, the teacher, and each other. With a new-found focus on content, rather than on technology, peer discussions can be elevated to more rewarding exchanges, such as: "Yes, John, you need to draw the line *here* in order to bisect the angle. Let's finish our sketch so we can send it to the teacher to show to the class. I think we are going to get it right!"

Hardware Features for 1-to-1 Tablet PC Deployments

In this section we consider features of tablet PC hardware in the context of 1-to-1 tablet PC deployments. In particular, we look at the pros and cons of convertibles and slates in a 1-to-1 deployment, as well as the advantages of smaller devices.

Convertibles Versus Slates

Experience from several 1-to-1 tablet PC deployments suggests that students will use the tablets in varied modes during class, depending on the task at hand. In some situations, students will want to use the keyboard to interact with the tablet PC; while in other situations, students will want to use the pen.

> For a detailed overview of tablet PC hardware, see "The Tablet PC: A Machine for Every Occasion" in chapter 1.

Keeping these diverse usage patterns in mind can be useful when comparing tablet PC models. Most tablet PCs fall into one of two primary forms: convertible and slate.

Convertible

The convertible looks like a standard laptop and comes complete with an attached keyboard (Fig. 6.1). In addition to using the keyboard, the user can draw on the screen of the tablet PC with a special pen. Because a convertible tablet PC screen is attached to its keyboard via a swivel pivot (instead of via a hinge, as is typical for laptops), a tablet PC screen can be twisted and positioned to lie flat on top of the keyboard. Thus the tablet PC can be converted into a device that allows the user to write on the tablet PC screen as easily as she or he would write on a paper notebook.

FIGURE 6.1. | The convertible form of a tablet PC

Many students and teachers have noticed an unanticipated benefit while using a convertible style tablet PC in a 1-to-1 environment. The swivel screen makes it easy for a student to share work with others. It is common to see a student twist his or her display toward a peer during a collaborative activity. Similarly, students can swivel their screens toward a teacher who is standing nearby to offer advice or to check work.

Slate

The slate is an alternative to the convertible tablet PC. Whereas the convertible tablet PC has an integrated keyboard, the slate tablet PC comes with an external keyboard, which is attached via a cable or docking station (Fig. 6.2). Because there is no permanently attached keyboard, slate models tend to be lighter than convertibles.

FIGURE 6.2. | A slate form of a tablet PC

Convertibles tend to be more popular in situations where users make regular use of both the keyboard and pen. Because students tend to use both the keyboard and the pen during class, the convertible tends to be preferred for student use in 1-to-1 tablet PC deployments.

A Matter of Size

In some circles, the notion of 1-to-1 implies that each student has long-term possession of a computer—over the course of a year or longer. In less strict definitions, each student may be provided with a computer to use only during a particular class. Tablet PCs may be permanently housed in a classroom, or they may be shuttled among rooms on specialized carts that also serve as charging stations (Fig. 6.3).

Which of these deployment models you use may have some impact on the size of the device you select. Tablet PCs typically vary in diagonal screen size from approximately 10 to 14 inches. Smaller (and lighter) units may be advantageous if younger students need to carry the devices regularly between home and school.

FIGURE 6.3. | 1-to-1 deployment of tablet PCs can involve sharing the computers among different classes.

Smaller devices also have a somewhat surprising advantage when used in a 1-to-1 deployment (Fig. 6.4). Anyone who has taught in a standard computer laboratory full of large displays knows that, due to the visual barrier the screens present, the teacher can feel disconnected from the students. Making eye contact with students who are often hidden behind large monitors can be difficult, especially in classes with younger, smaller students.

Regardless of their size, all tablet PCs provide a line-of-sight advantage (as compared to a laptop) when the tablet is lying flat in pen-input mode. However, smaller tablet PCs continue to provide this advantage even when the screen is positioned vertically to facilitate typing.

FIGURE 6.4. | Smaller screen size provides a line-of-sight advantage in the class-
room and helps maintain teacher–student engagement.

Software for 1-to-1 Tablet PC Deployments

The full educational potential of 1-to-1 tablet PC deployments is realized through the use of software applications that exploit the power of the pen. We will examine general productivity tools, as well as show examples of collaboration and content-specific software and their uses.

Some of these applications can be classified as general productivity tools, while others are designed specifically for an educational environment. This latter group of software can be further divided into software systems that are tied to particular content areas and those systems that support the teaching and learning process across disciplines.

1-to-1 Classroom Uses of General Productivity Tools

In the context of this section, a general productivity tool is a software system that is useful to teachers and students even though it was not designed specifically as an educational application.

> For a detailed look at how the tablet PC can enhance personal productivity for students and teachers alike, see chapter 4, "Personal Productivity for Classroom Teachers."

The most well-known general purpose productivity tool that can be used naturally in a 1-to-1 tablet PC deployment is Microsoft Word. When Word senses that it is running on a tablet PC, it enables additional inking features that allow ink annotations to be made on top of typed text.

Microsoft OneNote is a more pen-centric example of a general productivity tool for the tablet PC. The basic functionality of this application allows the user to take, organize, and search freehand notes, typed notes, or a combination of the two. Significantly more support for digital ink is provided in OneNote as compared to Word. This enhanced ink functionality can be useful in settings ranging from business meetings to classrooms, especially when the subject matter lends itself to sketches and diagrams.

During class, students can use Word or OneNote, instead of paper and pencil, to take notes. The resulting electronic notebooks have several advantages over paper notebooks. They are more easily searchable, they can be organized efficiently, and they can be submitted easily to the teacher for review and comment after class. OneNote provides some particularly nice organization and search capabilities, including the ability to search digital ink and the ability to easily flag certain topics in a notebook for later search.

Classroom Uses of Content-Specific Applications

This section discusses applications that focus on a specific content area. These applications can be used during class to help students become engaged with the material.

The sampling of applications presented here is meant to illustrate the range of software available while suggesting ways they can be used to engage students in a 1-to-1 tablet PC deployment.

The following two examples are available as part of a freely downloadable collection of programs called Microsoft PowerToys for Windows XP Tablet PC Edition.

> For a detailed look at tablet PC software as they relate to personal productivity, see "Software Features: The Power of the Pen" in chapter 4.
>
> For a detailed look at tablet PC software as they relate to single-user classroom settings, see "Curriculum-Specific Software and Uses" in chapter 5. Also see chapter 3, "Key Resources."

Physics Illustrator

As the name implies, Physics Illustrator enables teachers and students to draw freehand sketches of simple scenarios and objects in the physical world (Fig. 6.5). Objects such as inclined planes, springs, strings, rods, and weights are easily drawn. The user can also sketch forces that will act on these objects. The software recognizes the objects and applies the specified forces to them, resulting in an animated scenario that helps students understand the principles of the physics involved. Students can also carry out "what if" explorations by changing, for example, the mass of an object or the size of a spring to see the impact of their changes.

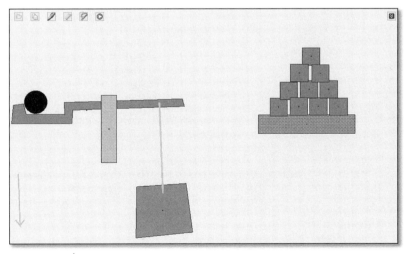

FIGURE 6.5. | Physics Illustrator in action.

During class, students can work in pairs to carry out experiments. For example, the students can be asked to predict how changing an input parameter (such as the direction of the wind) will affect a simulated system. After students record their predictions, they can use the system to test their predictions.

Writing Practice Tool

This fun and engaging program encourages young students to practice writing words in freehand. After a student writes a word, the ink strokes drawn by the student are auto-transformed into a sketch of that word. For example, if the student traces over the word "flower," the ink will be transformed into a sketch of a flower (Fig. 6.6).

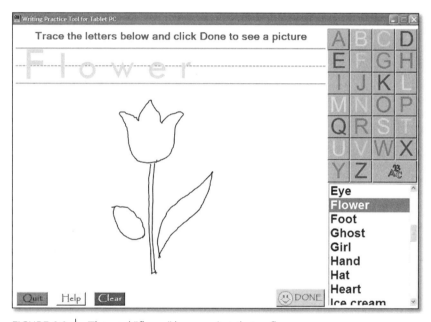

FIGURE 6.6. | The word "flower" becomes just that—a flower.

Teachers can easily add new words and pictures to the system, thus providing students with an unlimited customized set of words. Teachers can move throughout the room, coaching students as they practice their writing. Because the system is highly interactive, it easily holds the interest of students even when the teacher is not directly working with them.

Cross-Discipline Classroom Interaction Tools

In the context of a 1-to-1 program, some pen-enabled educational software systems are designed to support the teaching and learning process across content areas. DyKnow Vision, Classroom Presenter, and Ubiquitous Presenter are examples of this type of software.

Although these applications can be used in a traditional 1-to-1 laptop program, they fit especially well into a 1-to-1 tablet PC program. We will focus on one of these applications, DyKnow Vision, because it is a fully-supported, scalable solution that has been broadly used from kindergarten through high school, as well as in higher education.

When using DyKnow Vision, the teacher can extemporaneously draw sketches on a tablet PC or on another pen-based input device (such as an electronic whiteboard). The teacher can also use a convertible tablet PC (or a standard notebook computer) to type material and then import prepared content, including PowerPoint slides and live Web pages. All information sketched, typed, or imported by the teacher appears immediately on each student's display. Each student can use a keyboard or pen to make private annotations to the teacher's material.

A variety of features in this software can be used to promote student engagement and help them make the transition from "transcribers" to "thinkers." To promote discussion, portions of one (or more) of the student workspaces can be viewed by the teacher or shared with the entire class. Alternatively, students can engage in multiple-choice polls, participate in focused chat sessions, or "draw on the board" from his or her seat. To encourage peer-to-peer collaboration and problem-solving skills, the teacher can also assign the students into work groups, such that students within each group share virtual sheets of paper.

Web pages containing interactive activities can also be embedded in the DyKnow notebook and then shared with the class. Using the companion DyKnow Monitor software, teachers can isolate the focus for student attention by blanking nonrelevant student screens or by limiting student access to select programs or Web sites.

DyKnow Vision and other similar software packages support in-class activities that both encourage sharing and promote discussion. Teachers in lower grades have used DyKnow Vision to transmit vocabulary words to the class where students then work alone or in pairs to write sentences using these words. Selected student work can then be shared with the class, and the student authors can be asked to stand and read their sentences aloud.

A similar pedagogy can be used in a higher-level mathematics class. For example, a set of practice problems can be drawn or typed by the teacher and then transmitted to the class (Fig. 6.7). Again, students can work alone or in pairs to solve these problems before sharing their solutions with the class. This type of instruction is applicable to almost any subject area. To name a few, students can write sentences in a foreign language class, fill in a time line in a history class, identify metaphors in an English class, and draw molecules in a chemistry class. In each case, work completed by one or more students can be viewed privately by the teacher or shared with the class to promote discussion.

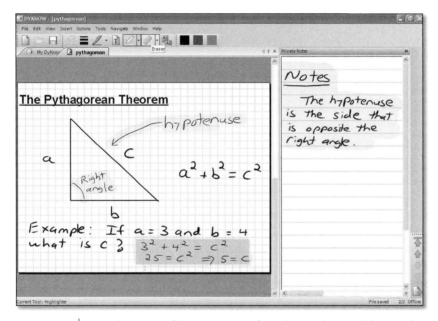

FIGURE 6.7. | A student's view of the DyKnow interface. The typed text and the triangle were prepared by the teacher before class. When the teacher imported this panel during class, these objects appeared on each student's display.

Figure 6.7 illustrates the collaborative nature of this software. As the teacher explained the Pythagorean theorem, she made annotations, all of which were transmitted to each student's display in real time. In this case, the teacher labeled the three sides of the triangle with "a," "b," and "c." Students also made some private annotations. Some of these annotations were integrated into the teacher's drawing in the left pane, while others were made in a separate Private

Notes window shown in the right pane. All of the students' annotations have been highlighted for clarity.

Finally, along the bottom of the left pane, the teacher has posed a question that asks the students to determine the value of "c" under the assumption that "a" is 3 and "b" is 4. The students' collective work is shown just below the problem statement. The teacher could choose to view this work privately or share it with the class to promote discussion.

At the end of class, each student can save or print his or her personalized electronic notebook that includes all of the teacher's content, all of the students' private annotations, and the results of any in-class interactions that the teacher has chosen to share with the class. While studying, these notes can be replayed stroke by stroke, allowing students to review class work in a dynamic manner. This is a particularly helpful feature in disciplines that use graphs and diagrams that evolve over time.

Because these documents are digital, blank and completed documents can be distributed electronically. For example, an instructor can distribute a quiz in the morning, receive the completed documents during the day, annotate them with feedback and assign a grade, and then return them to the student.

DyKnow Vision has been used in a broad range of grade levels, extending from kindergarten through graduate school, and has enhanced the classroom experience in subject areas such as mathematics, writing, economics, physics, history, and Japanese language.

TABLET PCS IN THE REAL WORLD

DyKnow Vision in Action

Mr. Jackson is showing his geometry class how to use the Pythagorean theorem to compute the length of the hypotenuse of a right triangle with the help of DyKnow software tools. To begin, Mr. Jackson works a sample problem by drawing a triangle on his tablet PC and illustrating how to apply the theorem. Everything he draws appears instantly on each of his student's tablet PCs.

Because Mr. Jackson has blocked the students from running any other programs, he is confident that they are focused on his lesson. As Mr. Jackson explains the process of using the theorem, students use their pens to make personalized notes alongside the content that Mr. Jackson is drawing on their screens.

Mr. Jackson glances at his student-status indicator and sees that 75% of the class has indicated that they do not understand his explanation fully. Based on this, Mr. Jackson works through a second sample problem to reinforce the concept.

Mr. Jackson transmits three practice problems to his class. He arranges the students in pairs, using the DyKnow software, so that each pair of students is sharing a work area. He then asks each pair to collaborate and solve the practice problems. The noise level rises and as Mr. Jackson moves through the room to coach students as needed, he can hear that their conversations are on-task.

John and Mary have been assigned to work as a pair. As John begins to sketch a solution to the problem on his screen, everything he does is immediately displayed on Mary's screen. Mary realizes that John has mislabeled the hypotenuse. As she explains the mistake to John she draws the correction which immediately appears on John's screen. John nods in agreement and the pair continues to work on the remaining problems.

After about 10 or 15 minutes, Mr. Jackson sees that John and Mary's work is coming along well, and he decides to share their work with the entire class. Sarah raises her hand and asks a question about both the solution and about John and Mary's work. As Mr. Jackson addresses these questions, he makes annotations on his own tablet PC. These are again transmitted to the entire class, and the students choose to add their own comments to their notebooks based on Mr. Jackson's explanation.

Before the instructor can ask if there are any other questions, Scott says, "Lindsay and I understand this problem, but we were not sure how to do the second one. We started to work on it, but then we got stuck. Can you pull up our answer?" Mr. Jackson shares Scott and Lindsay's solution with the class and, when prompted, Michael constructively points out their error. Scott and Lindsay quickly correct their mistake and finish the problem. The bell rings and each student saves a personalized copy of the electronic notebook for after-class study, review, and replay.

Research: Impact of 1-to-1 Tablet PC Deployments

Published research on the impact of 1-to-1 tablet PC deployments in K–12 settings range from descriptions of relatively straightforward teacher observations to larger assessments involving external evaluators.

Recent examples can be found in the publications resulting from the recent Workshop on the Impact of Pen-Based Technology on Education (WIPTE) conference (www.itap.purdue.edu/tlt/conference/wipte/).

> For a summary of some key issues related to 1-to-1 tablet PC deployment at an organizational level, please see the Challenges for 1-to-1 Deployment boxes in chapter 7.

An article in *T.H.E. Journal* (Schroeder, 2004) presents the experiences of a mathematics teacher who deployed tablet PCs and DyKnow Vision at Cabrillo High School in Lompoc, California. The author writes: "I used DyKnow [Vision] on the tablet PCs in my Math II class, a two-semester mathematics course, [during the 2003–2004 academic year. Mainly geared toward sophomores, the course becomes progressively harder by the second semester, as more abstract topics are introduced. Using DyKnow [Vision] in Math II, second-semester final exam averages improved from 72% to 82% between the 2002–2003 and 2003–2004 academic years."

An evaluation of a larger 1-to-1 tablet PC deployment at the Vermont Academy (Payton, 2006) focused on the use of GoBinder as a tool to support student note taking and organization. A survey was administered to students who had used GoBinder in order to determine whether they found value in specific uses of the system. Twenty survey respondents had used GoBinder to keep track of assignments. Of these, 16 believed the system was more useful than paper and pencil for this task. Many students also found value in using GoBinder both as a scheduling and a note-taking tool. For more details, see the case study, "Vermont Academy: The Personal Productivity of Students," in chapter 4 (p. 81).

An interesting evaluation (Sommerich, 2007) has resulted from a partnership between Bishop Hartley High School in Columbus, OH, and its neighbor The Ohio State University. Approximately 240 junior and senior high school students who participated in a 1-to-1 tablet PC program were invited to take part in a study conducted by researchers from The Ohio State University. Of the eligible students, 106 consented to participate in the study. Data was collected from participants via a two-part written survey that asked about tablet PC usage patterns and related ergonomic factors. Additional data was collected from a smaller subset of 13 students over 16 consecutive days via a software logging program that captured the amount of time students spent using the tablet PC keyboards and digital pens. The researchers found that the tablet PCs were heavily used by the students, with more than 90% of the students reporting regular use of the devices for each of the following tasks: "writing notes, typing notes, typing papers, accessing the Internet, and accessing class notes."

The researchers also found that students vary their choice of input modality based on the task at hand. Specifically, "Over 90% of the students used the writing stylus and the keyboard when using the TPC to take notes; whereas when using the TPC for papers, over 90% used the keyboard, but only 26% used the stylus." Generally, the students reacted very positively to the tablet PCs, although there were concerns raised about distractions in class and about visual and musculoskeletal discomfort.

In another study involving an external evaluation team (Sloan, 2006), researchers from the Web site Rockman et al (www.rockman.com) evaluated the use of tablet PCs and DyKnow Vision software in a sixth-grade mathematics class at North Daviess Elementary School in Elnora, Indiana. The researchers observed students in class who were using this technology to study the mathematical concepts of counting, rounding, and cost-comparison in the context of comparing four brands of chocolate chip cookies. The researchers also interviewed teachers and reviewed test scores.

The researchers reported that the students were engaged throughout the class and that they were comfortable using the hardware and software. They further reported that their interviews suggest that students' note-taking and study skills improved because the teacher could share examples of good notes with the class. Teachers also reported that learning gains were especially prominent among students with special needs.

TABLET PCS IN THE REAL WORLD

Bishop Hartley High School

Partnering with Higher Education to Assess a 1-to-1 Tablet Deployment

Bishop Hartley High School, a private school in Columbus, Ohio, pioneered 1-to-1 tablet PC computing when it gave a tablet PC to each of the 150 students in its senior class in the spring of 2003. Today, 500 students from Bishop Hartley and partner high school Bishop Watterson are involved in a 1-to-1 tablet PC initiative. The aggressive tablet programs at these schools are supported by the Columbus Diocesan as part of an overall focus on using technology to support teaching and learning.

Bishop Hartley students use Hewlett-Packard TC1100 and TC4200 tablet PCs in all of the core disciplines. Key software packages include Microsoft Journal, Art Rage, Audio Notes Recorder, DyKnow Vision, and DyKnow Monitor. Uses include electronic painting in art class; recording audio notes in foreign language classes; test review, note sharing and support for debating in government class; and the illustration of battles in a military history class.

Informal evaluation shows that this tablet PC program has been well received. Foreign Language teacher Fulvia Fowler said, "My favorite feature is being able to assign oral lessons that students can complete and return to me in oral or handwritten form. I am able to test listening, speaking skills, as well as writing proficiency with all associated language accents."

Social studies chairperson Curt Hanson also has strong positive feelings about the impact the tablet PCs have had on the student experience. In a video produced by Bishop Hartley Students, Hanson notes: "With DyKnow, it is easy to give notes to the students by giving them prompts and questions that they can complete." He also sees great benefit in using the system to provide students with links to course-related Web sites and resources. The video can be found at www.dyknow.com/community/students.aspx; click What Students are Saying to reveal the Bishop Hartley School link (.wmv file).

To carry out a more formal evaluation of their tablet PC program, technology leaders at Bishop Hartley are partnering with researchers at The Ohio State University (OSU). The partnership began when employees at a local research company read about Bishop Hartley's tablet PC initiative. The research company had ties to OSU and introduced Ken Collura, Director of Communications and Instructional Technology for the Columbus Diocesan Department of Education, to faculty who were interested in tablet PC research. After several meetings, the partners were able to specify a research project that was mutually beneficial.

When asked about the benefits that the research collaboration brings to Bishop Hartley, Collura said, "[The partnership] gives validity and credibility to the research. You can always do internal studies, but when a study comes along with the credentials of the Ohio State University, it gives the information real credibility...We always want to evaluate if the technology we invest in is enhancing the learning experience for students on the individual level. That determines if the program is successful, and the OSU partnership gives me the ability to see if that goal was achieved."

Although the research project is ongoing, Collura reports that he has already received some positive results. For example, he says the researchers have learned that "some student groups, like the junior and senior girls, are more likely to participate in class [ever] since they have adopted tablets." OSU researcher Dr. Carolyn Sommerich has plans for continuing her work with Bishop Hartley. "During the first two years of the study, we focused on observation," Dr. Sommerich explained, "watching and analyzing how the students used the tablet PC. This year we introduced intervention into our study. Our plan is to continue with this two-pronged study for the next few years."

Bishop Hartley was a leader in deploying tablets in the spring of 2003. Now they are leading the way toward showing how K–12 schools and neighboring higher-education institutions can work together to carry out meaningful assessments.

TABLET PCS IN THE REAL WORLD

Auburn City Schools

A Model Faculty Development Program in the Context of a 1-to-1 Tablet Deployment

Auburn City Schools, in Auburn, AL, had approximately 400 Gateway M285 Convertible tablet PCs deployed to ninth-grade students during the 2006–2007 academic year. An additional 450 tablets were ordered for the 2007–2008 school year. Approximately 60 junior high teachers and 80 high school teachers have tablets.

Tablets are fully integrated into the delivery of Auburn's curriculum, with all core classes (math, science, language arts, social studies, art, and music) making use of them. These curricular uses are supported by a number of software packages that are installed on every tablet PC in the 1-to-1 program. These packages include Microsoft Office, DyKnow Vision, DyKnow Monitor, electronic textbooks, Geometer's Sketchpad, and software such as PassKey, which is licensed by the state and used to prepare students for the standard exit exam.

Auburn's transition to a 1-to-1 tablet PC program is notable for its thoughtful approach to faculty development. Tablet PCs were given to ninth-grade teachers a full year before they were given to the students. This gave the teachers ample time to adjust to the new technology before having to use it in a 1-to-1 environment. An analysis of teacher needs conducted during the year-long transition period showed that—once the 1-to-1 program was rolled out—teachers were most concerned about finding ways to integrate the new technology into the classroom in meaningful ways.

To help teachers overcome this hurdle, they were asked to attend a weekly 60-minute "Technology Tuesday" training session.

According to Debbie Rice, Director of Technology for Auburn City Schools, Auburn's faculty development program remained centered on teacher needs as the year progressed. At the end of each "Technology Tuesday" session, teachers provided written feedback that was used to determine the topics to be covered in the following week.

To further focus the training sessions on authentic faculty needs, the training team had teachers bring their own documents and lesson plans to the "Technology Tuesday" sessions. The team showed the teachers how they could enhance their existing materials and improve the learning experience for their students by integrating technology-based methods. For example, teachers learned how to make documents accessible to students from Web sites, and they learned how to transmit their content to students (and to receive answers from students) using DyKnow tools. The focus on teachers quickly generated a solid buy-in.

When the 1-to-1 initiative launched, the dedication to teacher development paid off through many positive teaching and learning experiences. In reflecting on her first year teaching in a 1-to-1 paradigm, a language arts teacher wrote, "This year has been very rewarding as well as very exciting for me... it is great to see how students are so engaged in learning each day. They tend to stay on task and their organization skills have improved as well. Overall, my class averages have improved. Most importantly, the discipline problems have drastically decreased...I think the students are excited to know there are fun and creative ways to learn. They are engaged in the lesson each day; therefore, [this] does not leave any room for disruption or behavior problems."

Future Directions

Over the past few years, several hardware peripherals that started out as options for high-end laptops have become mainstream components for all laptops. It wasn't too long ago that users paid extra for color screens (this type of display is now standard). The same can be said for integrated wireless cards and CD/DVD drives.

Mainstreaming of Tablet PC Devices in 1-to-1 Deployments

Over the next few years, it seems likely that all laptops will include pen-input technology. This transition is likely to be accelerated by two factors: the drop in price of the hardware needed to support pen-based input, and the adoption of the Microsoft Vista operating system, which has better support for pen-input than previous Microsoft operating systems.

When the pen is fully integrated into the standard laptop, there will no longer be a discussion of (or a choice to be made between) 1-to-1 tablet PC deployments versus traditional 1-to-1 laptop deployments. Instead, all 1-to-1 mobile computing deployments will provide pen-based input capabilities, just like all such deployments now involve devices with color displays.

There will likely remain questions and discussions about the particular style of pen-based computing devices for use in 1-to-1 deployments. Questions in regard to device choice will come in terms of form factors, particularly with respect to size. For example, the new UMPC (Ultra-Mobile Personal Computer), which is typically larger than a PDA but smaller than a tablet PC, may play an increasingly important role in 1-to-1 deployments. This will especially be true when UMPC prices drop. When priced competitively, the small size of UMPCs should prove to be especially attractive in 1-to-1 deployments involving younger students (who will find, among other things, the UMPC is easy to carry between home and school).

The Impact of 1-to-1 Programs on Distance Education

Once students and teachers are comfortable using tablet PCs in the classroom, creative uses can come naturally for extending the walls of the classroom. In fact, this is happening already. For example, when a teacher at Bishop Hartley High School (who was already using DyKnow Vision with her students) recently became ill, she was able to log into the class session remotely and teach from home, rather than cancel her class altogether. Her only accommodation was to have an assistant present in the classroom to help with class management. Other teachers have used a similar approach to conduct review sessions from remote locations.

Some schools are also discussing the use of tablet PCs as part of disaster preparedness planning, particularly for instances when (or if) an outbreak of an infectious disease makes it ill-advised for students to come to class. If tablet PCs, communication technologies, and appropriate supporting software are already in use to support in-class communication, it becomes relatively easy to continue their use at a distance. It should be noted that this strategy is much simpler than trying to put technology in place that will be used only in the event of an emergency. It would be truly chaotic to have students "attend" classes electronically if they had to rely on a technology that they were not already comfortable using in their own local setting.

Integration of Artificial Intelligence

Several researchers have been investigating ways that computer recognition of freehand input can be used to foster student learning. For example, the Tablet PC Math System can be used to give students feedback as they use electronic pens to solve simple arithmetic problems. When using the system, a student is presented with a sequence of problems. The student solves the problem using the digital pen to indicate "borrows" and "carries," as needed, and then inks the final answer into the interface. The software recognizes the freehand input, determines if the answer is correct, and provides immediate feedback. A Web-based administrative tool is also available to provide the teacher with student-performance reports. It is easy to imagine students in a 1-to-1 environment using this system to practice arithmetic. In this scenario, the system could be enhanced to alert the teacher which of the students' work contained errors, thus enabling the teacher to focus attention where it is needed most.

Classroom Learning Partner is a more ambitious example of ink recognition that may hold future promise. The long-term goal of this system is to analyze student responses to open-ended questions by grouping the responses into categories (Koile & Singer, 2006). For example, correct responses would be placed into one group; responses that exhibit a certain error would be placed into a second group; responses exhibiting a different error in a third group, and so on. When used in a 1-to-1 environment, this system would help the teacher quickly recognize the answer categories for a particular problem.

Staying Abreast

With the popularity of 1-to-1 tablet PC deployments increasing, several conferences and events are becoming recognized as good places to network with others who use Tablet PCs in their schools, and to stay up-to-date with current information and cutting-edge technologies.

The Laptop Institute

Hosted each summer by the Lausanne Collegiate School in Memphis, Tennessee, this event brings together upwards of 500 participants who are mostly educators from K–12 schools that have, or are considering, a 1-to-1 mobile PC deployment (www.laptopinstitute.com). This annual event started out focusing on 1-to-1 deployments of traditional laptops. The past three years have seen an increasing emphasis on 1-to-1 tablet PC deployments, and the trend is likely to continue.

"Tablets in the Classroom" Conference

Hosted three or four times each year by the Cincinnati Country Day School in Cincinnati, Ohio (www.countryday.net/tech/LALP/), this event is notable for its exclusive focus on 1-to-1 tablet PC deployments, as well as for its thoroughly hands-on nature. Participants are loaned a tablet PC at the start of each conference. They use the tablet PC to experience, first-hand, how teachers at this school are using this technology to engage students.

Workshop on the Impact of Pen-based Technology in Education (WIPTE)

Held annually at Purdue University in West Lafayette, Indiana (www.purdue.edu/wipte/), this event covers both K–12 and higher-education deployments of tablet PCs and other pen-based computing approaches. The workshop focuses particularly on the evaluation of the impact of these deployments. (Monographs containing the workshop presentation papers are published by Purdue University Press.)

7 | Deploying Tablet PCs in Your School

EDWARD J. EVANS
  IT Teaching and Learning Technologies
  Purdue University

IN THIS CHAPTER

- The critical reasons why a school should deploy tablet PCs

- The essential five steps for implementation

- Case study: Memorial Middle School

- Specific challenges for 1-to-1 deployments

Begin with the end in mind.

Educational institutions have long searched for the "ultimate" device and the next "killer application" that would produce transformational changes in the learning process. Throughout the search, products such as networked calculators, PDAs, and even notebook computers have been evaluated, incorporated and— ultimately—abandoned as that "killer" device. Technologists, faculty, and administrators continue their quest.

Enter the tablet PC.

Sorting Through the Issues

As noted in previous chapters, the tablet PC is a notebook computer that uses a Windows operating system and runs traditional software packages. It is a device that allows users to write directly onto its screen—an essential feature in classrooms that rely on hand-written notes, equations, symbols, tables, or charts. It is large enough to feature plenty of screen real estate, yet it is small enough to sit comfortably on a student's desk, much like a three-ring binder. Thought of in these ways, it becomes easy to understand why many believe the tablet PC to be *the* device that can transform teaching and learning.

But the hype surrounding tablet PCs is diminishing. Left behind are difficult questions about the value-added elements of pen-based computing for learning, as well as the financial implications of this relatively more-expensive computing platform. How does one sort through these (and many other) issues to find the answers required for a successful deployment of tablet PCs?

Begin with the end in mind.

> A good plan is like a road map: It shows the final destination and usually the best way to get there.
>
> —H. STANLEY JUDD

Develop a Roadmap

Planning is the only way to achieve a successful technology implementation, and it is critical to the long-term viability of a large-scale deployment.

These plans must clearly articulate the goals of the project. They must also identify the necessary steps and critical factors required for a successful tablet PC deployment. Finally, they should help all participants to understand "why" *before* any implementation occurs.

Indeed, why should a school or district choose to implement tablet PCs? There are a number of reasons; for example, to:

- Facilitate recruitment
- Aid marketing efforts

- Prepare students for a rapidly changing and increasing global world

- Encourage student cooperation

- Improve teacher–student communication

- Enhance curriculum

- Improve personal productivity

- Minimize the digital divide

- Promote deeper learning

Whatever the goals of a given tablet PC deployment, they must be clearly articulated. The result will help participants create a solid plan. And, in turn, a solid plan will keep all parties working toward the stated goals.

As discussed in previous chapters, different types of software and training are needed for improving personal productivity, as compared to improving student-teacher communications or enabling group work. Likewise, large 1-to-1 tablet PC deployments are much more difficult to support than teacher-only or cart-based deployments.

> First you write down your goal; your second job is to break down your goal into a series of steps, beginning with steps which are absurdly easy.
>
> —FITZHUGH DODSON

A well-thought-out plan also communicates the many changes that are required for implementing a tablet PC program. Often times, technology evangelists over-simplify the adoption of new technology. After all, it is as easy as procurement and distribution, right? Actually, seldom is this the case, particularly in larger institutional settings. Training programs must be developed, faculty must adapt, and infrastructure and support processes must be implemented. Without these critical pieces, a new technology program will flounder, even in the hands of the greatest technology enthusiast.

Developing a successful tablet PC implementation roadmap need not be difficult. It can be as simple as these five steps:

1. Find a partner

2. Identify faculty needs

3. Develop a mobile infrastructure

4. Promote assessment

5. Commit for the long haul

Find a Partner

A good vendor is more than simply a supplier of technology—a good vendor is a *partner* in your implementation. A partner is critical to a successful program. Even a minimal tablet PC program requires timely delivery of newly-purchased units, be it hardware or software. In the days of demand forecasts, global assembly, and distribution centers, even the task of order delivery becomes complex: Company forecasts can be wildly exceeded, and it can take longer than expected for manufacturers to assemble and deliver products from halfway around the globe.

It is always best to review multiple potential partners. The Gartner "Magic Quadrant for Global Enterprise Notebook PCs" (www.gartner.com) document provides valuable information on the major players in the notebook market, many of whom also carry tablet PCs. The Magic Quadrant provides indication of the reliability/stability of the vendor and their ability to service products they sell.

In considering the appropriate hardware and software to purchase from a partner, deployment and educational goals are important. In large-scale, multi-year deployments, it is also important to consider consistency-over-time models. This requirement may be less critical in smaller, course-based deployments. Regardless, the least expensive computer to purchase may *not* be the least expensive to own or maintain over the long term. A good partner will promptly help mitigate any problems that are discovered along the way, and will do the most to help support and maintain the units purchased.

TABLET PCS IN THE REAL WORLD

Memorial Middle School
Quality Counts—Partnership with HP

Memorial Middle School is a public school that serves students in grades 6–8 in Tampa, Florida. The school received an HP Technology for Teaching Grant for the 2005–06 school year. The HP grant was directly correlated to the school's technology goal; namely to give students opportunities to explore a variety of technologies.

As teachers and students used tablet PCs, LCD projectors, and digital cameras on a daily basis to teach, practice, and review, they discovered that the quality and compatibility of the equipment had made life a lot easier, thus better facilitating learning. This may seem like a small or trivial detail, but as one instructor said, "It is time-consuming and annoying to have pieces of equipment that require other pieces of equipment or software to work together as a presentation unit. Having all HP equipment made everything work flawlessly and nothing fell apart in the middle of a lesson."

The instructor went on to add, "We utilized the LCD projector every day. The tablet PC enabled us to write directly onto a lesson for those small mini-lessons; the mobility of the screen enlarged the viewing area for the students. Everything that was needed for any lesson could be loaded onto the tablet PCs. Even the SD card from the camera allowed us to show student work. Students were also able to present their own projects...."

"Tablet technology," the instructor continued, "which must have been made for teachers in mind, has made such a positive impact on our instructional techniques that we cannot imagine teaching without it—the tablet PC and LCD projector, especially—now that we have it. Many things have gone well in the program. We made a smooth transition from using materials from before to using the up-to-date materials from the grant. We have met as a team periodically to review and assess our progress with the grant and the unit lesson plans. The books and courses that were afforded us were useful in giving us ideas for lessons that used the equipment."

Said another instructor, "The HP grant has opened up new adventures for our team at school. Students and other teachers have been asking us to show them and teach them about the technology. We have also had the honor of speaking to the mayor and council in our town about projects using our HP technology."

John Haley, principal of Memorial Middle School, summed up his experience with the school's partnership with HP. "I was pleased to see how easily team members were able to merge curriculum needs and the use of technology to instruct students. The teachers on this team are all very innovative, and I knew that winning this grant was a huge success for them, but I did not know that they were so ready to implement new ways of instructing our students. I have watched the kids' eyes light up when images are presented on screen, and I could see that they were making learning connections while being instructed with this new technology. The use of technology has made a positive difference in the learning experiences of the kids and the instructional practices of the teachers."

Identify Faculty Needs

I once had a student employee who helped with technology evaluation and implementation. With each new application evaluated, his mantra was "Don't mess with my workflow!"

Faculty often have much the same sentiment. After all, they put a lot of effort into creating a quality class with good content for students. They also know that at least as much work will go into redeveloping their content as it did to originally create it. As a result, teachers more readily accept technologies that "don't mess with" their workflow, but instead allow them to continue doing things much as they always have.

The tablet PC and software packages such as DyKnow Vision are excellent examples of technologies that truly aid student learning but require minimal content redevelopment on the part of the instructor. In its simplest form, the tablet PC allows inking on PowerPoint slides (much like a traditional overhead projector). Taken a step further, DyKnow Vision enables interactive white boarding for an entire class.

But requiring change is not the only barrier to implementing tablet PCs. Donovan, Hartley, and Neal (2007) found that most teachers worried about the impact that laptops would have on them as an individual, in terms of time, planning, and instructional practices. It was only after these concerns were addressed (and teachers became more comfortable with the technology) that they became concerned with how to best facilitate learning, improve teacher effectiveness, and enter into collaboration with others.

In the case of 1-to-1 deployments, teachers must become comfortable with giving up some control of their classes. When students are empowered to interact freely with a world of literature and information, no longer will the instructor be the "sage on the stage." To teach most effectively in a 1-to-1 computing environment, instructors do well to encourage students to use this technology and embrace its promise of boundless information for research, writing, and interacting in new ways. This new "guide on the side" mindset is required not only to engage students but to teach new information-literacy skills—skills required for the success of today's students.

CHALLENGES FOR 1-TO-1 DEPLOYMENT

Teacher Training

Tablet PCs are likely to be unfamiliar to most teachers and students. Although the technology itself is easy to learn, mastering it requires some practice. For successful 1-to-1 deployment, instructors must be comfortable enough with the technology to help the students through the learning process. In addition, discovering the best pedagogical practices for using pen-based technology in a 1-to-1 environment can take time.

Strategies

- If teachers are initially uncomfortable with a proposed 1-to-1 tablet PC deployment, technology leaders should consider giving tablet PCs to teachers a few months in advance of making the devices available to students. This will give the teachers some time to get comfortable with the devices in a less-pressured context.

- Once the teachers have their tablet PCs, they still must practice the pedagogies and types of interactions that occur in a 1-to-1 tablet PC deployment. Technology leaders should encourage groups of teachers to bring their tablet PCs and meet together. Here, the teachers can work in groups or take turns playing the role of the students. The aim is to show teachers how interactive tablet PC technologies work, from both the view of the teacher and the student.

- Look for hardware and software that provides good training and support services. A good vendor will want your deployment to succeed. They will offer training and support services, including services specifically aimed at helping teachers learn how to use tablet PCs effectively in a 1-to-1 context. This may be accomplished through direct training of teachers or through a train-the-trainer model.

- Technology leaders should provide professional development opportunities that focus on what teachers want to learn. Leaders should ask teachers what they need to know and then provide opportunities for learning. The Auburn City Schools case study (detailed in chapter 6, page 131) provides a good example of this approach.

- Technology leaders should encourage teachers to attend conferences and workshops that focus on 1-to-1 tablet PC deployments. Teachers will not only learn about best practices from other schools, but will be privy to the newest developments in educational technologies. For suggestions of specific events, see chapter 3, "Key Resources.".

Develop a Mobile Infrastructure

When embarking on a tablet PC initiative, a mobile infrastructure is second only to faculty development. The mobile infrastructure must be in place to support the use of tablet PCs within the classroom—for use by students and teachers. Clearly, the type and complexity of the infrastructure will vary greatly, depending on the goals of the deployment. There are important considerations that must be understood when implementing the mobile infrastructure, including:

- Wireless access
- Delivery of course materials
- Personal versus institutional ownership
- Device support
- Application access

Wireless Access

Although wireless access is not a requirement for deploying tablet PCs, it is simply good practice. Wireless access provides a quick and easy way for users to go online, interact within the classroom, augment class discussion with real-time searches, and access the latest notes for the course. For a 1-to-1 implementation, wireless access becomes a necessity if students are regularly going to bring their tablet PCs to class, and if classroom engagement is to be maintained.

Class-based wireless access may be easy to establish, particularly with a cart system. Mounting a wireless access point to a cart and rolling it into the room makes for easy connections and instant gratification for a wireless network. However, such a deployment has its downside—it is a scarce resource that potentially must be shared among many different classes.

Limitations in wireless access may become prevalent in large-scale implementations. As a general rule, 20 to 30 people can use one wireless access point. With three usable channels in proximity to one another, 802.11b/g offers the ability to support sixty to ninety tablet PCs. 802.11a networks fare somewhat better, allowing eight usable channels on access points in proximity to each other, for a total of 160–240 tablet PCs in a given location. Because these numbers are inadequate for large-scale environments, companies such as Meru Networks (www.merunetworks.com) have begun developing technologies that aim to overcome these limitations.

CHALLENGES FOR 1-TO-1 DEPLOYMENT

Infrastructure

As is the case with any 1-to-1 mobile computing deployment, it is important to consider infrastructure issues in terms of supporting classroom instruction. There are also some specialized issues to consider with 1-to-1 tablet PC deployments, including the inadvertent loss of pens.

Strategies

- Technology leaders should perform broad-based wireless connectivity tests well in advance of the first day of classes. It is not enough to be certain that one or two tablet PCs connect to a wireless access point. Technology leaders must conduct trial runs with the same number of devices planned for actual deployment during class. Technology leaders should also partner with technology departments and hardware vendors to be certain that the required infrastructure is in place.

- Technology leaders need to consider power management issues as carefully as wireless issues. If students will use the tablet PCs all day, how will they be powered? Will extended-life batteries be purchased? Will there be battery charging stations? Will there be places to plug in the tablets? If students will start by using the tablet PCs in only a few classes each day, these issues may not be of immediate concern.

- Don't forget the pens. A tablet PC without a functioning pen is not a useful tablet PC! Technology leaders should consider purchasing spare pens as backup replacements for lost or broken ones. Better yet, in an agreement with a hardware vendor, technology leaders should request plenty of spare pens. In order to prevent accidental pen loss, IT leaders should consider tethering tablet pens directly to the tablet PCs.

Delivery of Course Materials

Particularly important in 1-to-1 tablet PC deployments is the delivery of course materials. These materials range from presentation notes to textbooks. Anecdotal feedback from students has indicated that, although they find using the tablet PC in 1-to-1 deployments highly beneficial, they are reluctant to carry (in addition to their normal load of textbooks, notebooks, and classroom materials) the four- to six-pound tablet computer. However, students are eager to make a "trade," and carry the tablet instead of these other bulky materials.

Faculty and instructional designers should consider how course materials can be digitized and made readily available through course management systems, Web sites, and other electronic distribution means.

CHALLENGES FOR 1-TO-1 DEPLOYMENT

Distractions

Students have daydreamed, passed notes, doodled, and thrown spit balls as long as there have been classrooms. Putting a tablet PC in the hands of each student will not automatically eliminate distracting behaviors, although it may provide different ways for the students to be distracted.

Strategies

- The basic premise is this: Students want to be engaged. The best way to combat distraction is to engage them with in-class problem solving and other active-learning techniques supported by a 1-to-1 tablet PC program.

- Be sure students understand *why* tablet PCs have been introduced into your class, and what you expect the students to do (and not do) with these PCs during class. Most teachers have policies about talking, eating, and late homework. It only follows that policies about electronic distractions should also be established and communicated to your students.

- Many K–12 teachers find it useful for a classroom interaction system to integrate classroom-control functionality. Classroom-control tools are designed to cut down on electronic distractions. Classroom-control functionality typically includes the ability to: limit the programs a student can run during class; limit student Web browsing to a selected list of Web sites; blank student screens as needed for focus; and monitor student activity and progress by viewing a thumbnail of each student's screen.

Although it is possible to use classroom-control software without simultaneously using software that encourages interaction, doing so is like taking away junk food without providing a nutritious alternative. It is far easier for students to buy-in to the positive use of software over software that prevents them from doing things.

Remember the basic premise: Students *want* to be engaged. Provide them with opportunities to do so at every turn by balancing your classroom interaction tools with your classroom control tools.

Personal Versus Institutional Ownership

There are (broadly) two options for device ownership when implementing tablet PCs: The tablet PC can be a personal purchase by the student, or the institution can purchase it. The choice is an important decision because it has implications for support, application access, and general responsibility for the technology. In either case, institutions often choose to bear at least some of the financial-aid burden in an effort to assist students who are unable to purchase the technology on their own.

Device Support

Regardless of whether tablet PCs are used as a teaching aid for instructors or as a tightly integrated 1-to-1 learning tool, device support is critical to success of a tablet PC program. The ability to resolve problems as they arise is a significant factor in teacher technology use (Penuel, 2006). Teachers simply will not use an unreliable device. In fact, they would rather have no device at all. As a result, it is important to have spare units, a convenient location for technology support and repair, and expeditious return of the repaired units.

Most vendors will supply a given number of spare "loaner" units, should a student or faculty device fail. Ratios of loaner units to purchased units can be negotiated up-front in the procurement process, even in situations where the units are personally (rather than institutionally) owned. In addition to loaner units, it may be appropriate to arrange with IT staff to provide "hot-spares" in the vicinity of critical classrooms or during crucial lessons. This allows a device to be efficiently traded out, should it become non-responsive at an inopportune time.

It's important to point out that large 1-to-1 implementations are more complicated and difficult to support than smaller classroom or course-based implementations. This may be true for a variety of reasons. Certainly, the more units in operation, the more likely a failure will occur. Beyond that, students are creative individuals, and some students will use their tablet PCs in ways never before imagined. If devices are personally owned, the institution will have to first decide what role it is comfortable playing in the support of individual devices. In the case of personal ownership, the institution may determine that the best path is to require the student to work directly with the vendor to obtain repairs on a malfunctioning device.

Application Access

A tablet PC without access to appropriate software for teaching and learning is only marginally useful. Robert Kozma makes the case that the difference computers make in learning is derived from the more frequent use of the computer (Penuel, 2006). The more accessible the applications, the more likely both students and faculty will spend time using—thereby becoming more familiar and comfortable with—the technology.

After the types of applications are identified for institutional or course-based tablet PC deployment, consideration must be given to licensing. Vendors are often willing to extend best-pricing offers on software purchases only to institutionally-owned machines. As a result, site licenses for software that were already in place may not be available to personally-owned equipment without violating the license agreement. Identifying critical applications before beginning the tablet PC deployment process may enable more time for reviewing current software agreements and requesting appropriate changes.

Promote Assessment

The only way to determine whether goals have been reached, and particularly whether learning has been impacted, is through assessment. In the early planning stages of the overall tablet PC program, it is important to plan for program assessment. Whether the assessment involves teachers, students, or a combination of both, assessments are critical to a program's success. Further, a good assessment program may also be critical in regard to receiving continued institutional support and for scaling-up a small program into an institution-wide endeavor.

Until recently, assessment has been an afterthought for technology initiatives such as a tablet PC deployment. To aid in assessment, and to provide a forum for sharing common experiences, a number of workshops have emerged. These efforts include:

- The Workshop on the Impact of Pen-based Technology on Education (WIPTE): www.purdue.edu/wipte/

- The First International Workshop on Pen-Based Learning Technologies (PLT): http://plt2007.ing.unict.it

- SRI International: http://ctl.sri.com/projects/displayProject.jsp?Nick=hpguide

These programs provide some insight into assessing the value of pen-based technologies for both K–12 and higher education. Often times K–12 researchers partner with higher education researchers to conduct studies and present the results at these workshops. These workshops also publish work done by others.

Commit for the Long Haul

Commitment breeds willingness. Time is required to learn tablet PC technology, redevelop course materials, and become comfortable with new teaching and learning paradigms. And the time and energy faculty and students are willing to invest into a successful tablet PC deployment is proportional to their perception of its importance and long-term benefits.

David Brown (2003) writes: "Only a small portion (about 25%) of the potential benefit from computers-in-education is [realized], until at least 85% of the students have access."

Tablet PCs must become as commonplace as books for teachers and students to readily identify with these devices and incorporate them into their classes. Indeed, students and teachers who have access to tablet PCs over multiple semesters (rather than only for a few moments in a class) will not only have the opportunity and desire to learn more about this technology, but will seek out new ways to use it effectively.

PART III
Lesson Plans

IN THIS SECTION

These lessons take advantage of the tablet PC's capabilities and illustrate how this technology can be used to enhance the classroom learning experience.

These learning activities cannot address the needs of every teaching situation. Take these lessons and modify them to fit your circumstances and needs.

Adding and Subtracting Fractions

MATHEMATICS • SPECIAL EDUCATION

Description

Working as a group, students map out the steps necessary for adding fractions with uncommon denominators and then simplify the answer. Using concept-mapping software, students use their own tablet PC or their personal digital assistant (PDA) device to map out the solution and then keep it for individual reference.

Lesson adaptations show how to use this strategy to teach other math concepts.

Objective

Using concept-mapping software, students will:

- talk about and document the steps necessary for solving a math problem, using the vocabulary that is specific to that type of problem.

Materials

- Tablet PCs
- Digital projector
- Personal digital assistant (PDA) device installed with concept-mapping software (one for each student; optional)
- Tablet PC software for:
  - Concept-mapping (e.g., Inspiration or Kidspiration)
  - Collaboration (e.g., DyKnow Vision; optional)
  - Word processing (e.g., Microsoft Word; optional)
  - Presentations (e.g., Microsoft PowerPoint; optional)

Procedures

1. Using the tablet PC and projector, introduce the task: Adding and subtracting fractions. In the concept-mapping software, the title of the lesson is the main topic.

2. Introduce a simple one- to three-step problem; for example: ¾ + ⅚ = ? Discuss the steps involved in setting up a fraction problem to begin adding or subtracting, choosing the least common multiple, recognizing an improper fraction, and simplifying/reducing the answer. If you have your lesson available as a Word or PowerPoint document, the inking capability of the tablet PC makes it easy to write out fractions and save them as part of the document. You can use different colors of ink to set the steps apart.

3. Have students describe each step to complete the problem. Encourage students to use discourse each step of the way, but do not initially tell the students how to work the problem. When encouraging discourse, it is important to support interaction among the group and talk about and agree on solutions without giving the answer. It is important to ask questions like, "Why?" and "How did you get that answer?" and "Explain your thinking and tell me about it."

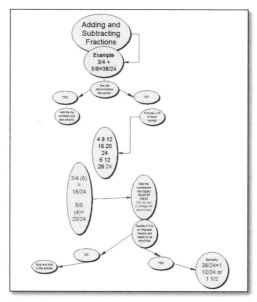

A completed graphic organizer using Inspiration.

4. Using only student input, model how to create the graphic organizer. This can also be accomplished using the pen and inking tools of the tablet PC.

Assessment

Each student completes a graphic organizer that describes the correct steps necessary to complete a particular math problem.

Adaptations. Early Primary, Grades 1–2

Whole Group. Presentation using tablet PC, concept-mapping software, and digital projector.

1. Main idea: What is addition?

2. Using the concept-mapping software, brainstorm meanings of addition, forming "bubbles" with each idea.

3. Lead the group until they understand the meanings of:

   a. More

   b. Adding together

   c. Getting bigger

4. Encourage discourse to decide when addition is encountered in real life and how it looks.

Individual Work. Provide each student with a blank template made in the concept-mapping software, complete with pre-made bubbles. The template should be in the same format as the one modeled in the Whole Group portion of the lesson:

1. Main idea: What is subtraction?

2. Pre-work the math and help students determine what classifications are needed, including:

   a. Take away

   b. Comparison

   c. Less

   d. Smaller number

3. Make sure the blank template has at least two more bubbles than necessary (to allow for "thinking outside the box" or alternative definitions).

Group Work. Students work in small groups to continue filling out the template.

Plenary. Group Share of ideas to fill in a class map on the tablet PC and projector.

Adaptations: Middle Primary, Grades 2–4

Whole Group. Presentation using tablet PC, concept-mapping software, and digital projector.

1. Main idea: What is multiplication?

2. To spark a discussion on the basics of multiplication, pose questions such as: What is multiplication? Where is it used? How is it used? What is the purpose of multiplication? Student ideas from this discussion will be recorded in the "bubbles."

3. Make sure to cover:

    a. multiplying is a way of counting faster

    b. adding "multiple" groups/sets together

    c. different types of visual representations of multiplication (arrays, groups, sets, etc.)

4. Ask leading/prompting questions to encourage student discourse to decide when multiplication is encountered in real life and how it looks.

Individual Work. Provide each student with a blank template created in the concept-mapping software, complete with pre-made bubbles. It should be in the same format as the one modeled in the Whole Group portion of the lesson:

1. Main idea: What is multiplication?

2. Pose the question to the students again: What is multiplication? Have students attempt to explain this using the template. Encourage them to use a multiplication problem to explain the concept by walking through the process of solving the problem and recording their thoughts in the bubbles.

3. Make sure to cover:

   a. multiplying is a way of counting faster

   b. adding "multiple" groups/sets together

   c. different types of visual representations of multiplication (arrays, groups, sets, etc.)

Pair Share/Group Work. Have students work in small groups to finish filling out their individual templates. Encourage students to discuss similarities and differences, and to share their observations with each other.

Closure/Summary of Concept. Use projector and software like DyKnow Vision to enable students to share their templates. Allow for group discussion of similarities and differences. Create a class map of the ideas from all the students. Discuss.

Review. Discuss and add necessary materials to the completed class map.

Adaptations: Higher Primary, Grades 5–6

Whole Group. Presentation using tablet PC, concept-mapping software, and digital projector.

1. Main idea: Change forms between fractions, decimals, and percents.

2. Given the fraction ⅕, create "bubbles" with a decimal and a comparable percent. Show several equal solutions, perhaps ending with the simplest form.

3. Lead the group for understanding of:

   a. Denominator

   b. Numerator

   c. Percent

   d. Simplest form

4. Encourage discourse to decide when the fraction, decimal, or percent is most appropriate for a situation. For instance, we often use ¾ of a teaspoon instead of 75% of a teaspoon.

Individual Work. Provide each student with a blank template made in the concept-mapping software, complete with pre-made bubbles. The template should be in the same format as the one modeled in the Whole Group portion of this lesson:

1. Main idea: Choose a fraction, decimal, or percent from the ones given; then recreate the steps in changing forms.

2. In the computer lab (or on the students' tablet PCs in a 1-to-1 environment), students insert text boxes to highlight the situations that are appropriate for the given examples. Students then complete the form and print it out.

3. Score the final template for accuracy. It should show at least two comparable examples for each form chosen.

More Ideas

Whereas Geometer's Sketchpad software is useful for visualization of mathematical concepts, Winplot can dynamically draw curves and surfaces. And while TI InterActive shows an on-screen calculator, MathJournal, MathPad, and FluidMath recognize and interpret mathematical sketches and formulas. The Tablet Math system can be used to give students feedback as they use digital pens to solve simple arithmetic problems.

National Educational Technology Standards for Students

1.c; 2.a, d; 3.a; 5.b

Animals of North America

SCIENCE, MATHEMATICS • GRADES K—2

Description

This lesson explores the appearance, motion, growth, and basic needs of animals in North America. Becoming virtual zoologists, students research, collect, and report data on the various animals of Canada, Mexico, and the United States. Students begin their exploration in the Canadian wilderness, go south to Mexico, and end their journey in the United States. The student zoologists study four animals in each country visited. Animal research is conducted using Internet resources, Knowledge Box, PBS video streaming, and virtual field trips to zoos and wilderness parks.

To support and guide their journey, teachers and students use a variety of technology, including tablet PCs, digital projectors, interactive whiteboards, digital cameras, scanners, printers, and the Internet. The tablet PC, in conjunction with the digital projector, allows teachers and students to compile notes and drawings in an interactive environment. Digital cameras and scanners allow students to record and document their journey along with adding visual aspects to the final presentation. Each group is in charge of presenting their findings to the other expert groups in the form of a multimedia presentation. This information is compiled into a culminating multimedia project, which incorporates PowerPoint or a digital portfolio.

Objectives

What students will know and be able to do is embedded in the science and math objectives, with additional objectives in reading, social studies, and writing. Students will:

- learn vocabulary associated with the appearance, motion, growth, and basic needs of animals in North America.

- define the characteristics and needs of animals in North America. They will compare and describe appearance, motion, growth and basic needs.

- learn and know where to find pertinent information regarding the topic, as well as how to present that information in a multimedia presentation. Teamwork and team dynamics will be emphasized.

- raise questions about the world around them and seek answers to questions by making observations and collecting data to draw conclusions. As a result, students will understand how animals are an integral part of our ecosystem, and they will express their views on the conservation of animals in North America.

- incorporate mathematics through the development of computation and estimation skills necessary for analyzing data and following the rules of scientific inquiry. Tools and instruments for observing, measuring, and graphing data will be used.

- recognize that North America is made up of three separate countries—Mexico, the United States of America, and Canada.

- gain an understanding of each country's climate, as well as the topographical and geographic similarities and differences of these three countries.

- demonstrate their ability to comprehend their research and synthesize it into logical, written thoughts by reading and compiling information from various resources and reporting that information in the form of notes, lists, journals, and data.

Materials

- Tablet PCs or an interactive whiteboard system
- Digital projector
- Scanner
- Digital camera
- Activote software (www.prometheanworld.com) or similar (optional)
- Internet access
- Printed materials—fiction and nonfiction books about various types of animals
- Video: *National Geographic*'s "Really Wild Animals: Amazing North America"

- Online encyclopedia (for animal research)
- Tablet PC software for:
    - Word processing (e.g., Microsoft Word)
    - Database spreadsheets with graphing capabilities (e.g., Microsoft Excel)
    - Presentations (Microsoft PowerPoint)
    - Drawing (e.g., Ambient Design's ArtRage; optional)

Essential Question

1. Why is it important to know the appearance, motion, growth, and basic needs of animals?

Unit Questions

1. What are the basic needs of animals?

2. What can we do to protect animals?

Content Questions

1. Where is North America located?

2. What are the characteristics of different animals?

3. How do we collect and organize data?

Preparation and Planning

Prior to beginning the unit, review objectives and information pertaining to animal characteristics, habitats, and basic needs. A general vocabulary list should be generated. A model of the end product should also be created. Technology equipment or lab times should be reserved.

Vocabulary. Students will keep a vocabulary journal so they can track the new vocabulary they learn. Keep a list of the vocabulary and definitions on the interactive whiteboard system or tablet PC for the class to review regularly. Students copy definitions from the teacher's chart and draw and color pictures to represent each vocabulary word. Using ArtRage on the tablet PC, students can easily save and share their artwork.

Prerequisite Skills. Students will need assistance creating PowerPoint presentations prior to beginning this unit or during the first week. Prior experience with searching the Internet is necessary. This skill should be reviewed in small groups or by using the tablet PC and projector or interactive whiteboard. Basic word processing skills are beneficial but not necessary; students with slower keyboarding skills may take advantage of the pen and inking capability of the tablet PC.

Procedures

Week One. To begin the unit, show students a variety of animals on a whiteboard flipchart (or use a tablet PC and projector). Discuss how the animals are all different and how they are the same. Brainstorm a list with a T-chart, using the interactive whiteboard. Have students fill out the "Know" part of a Know-Wonder-Learn (K-W-L) chart. Students can write words or draw pictures to represent what they know. After students have been given enough time to fill out the Know section of their chart, have them give you their ideas as you record them on the class K-W-L chart. Use their responses as a means for discussion along the way.

Spark students' curiosity by asking the question: What more do you want to know about the animals of North America? Have students fill out the "Wonder" section of their K-W-L chart. Give students time to fill out their chart. Bring the group back together and have students share their questions. Record them on the Wonder section of the class K-W-L chart. Keep the K-W-L chart posted for students to see throughout the unit. Make sure to come back to the questions as they are answered during the unit.

Present the Essential Question: Why is it important to know the appearance, motion, growth, and basic needs of animals? Using the whiteboard or a tablet PC with a projector, display this question for the class whenever they're working on this lesson. As students arrive at answers, they can ink those answers creatively around the question.

Students should also begin a storyboard journal. Within the journal, the students will collect pictures, drawings, and information they would like to include in their final project. If students create their storyboard journals within Microsoft Word or PowerPoint, they can draw or ink annotations directly onto the documents. By collecting the information in a storyboard, students will have the necessary information to include in their final presentation. In addition, teachers will be able to track progress and make adjustments as needed.

Week Two. Review continents and the location of North America. Prompt a discussion about the weather and landforms. Generate a list of what general types of animals might be found in these conditions. Offer the question: Do you think the animals in North America are the same as animals on other continents? Provide students with a list of animals that are generally found in North America. Have students choose an animal and decide whether to work in teams or individually.

Research time. Support teams and individuals as they spend the week researching questions about animals of North America. Brainstorm a list of everything that can be researched, such as size, lifespan, biome, habitat, habits, diet, growth, development, and whether a particular species is endangered. Use the tablet PC, digital projector, and Internet to model and demonstrate expected behaviors and research strategies.

Students should study their topic using cooperative experts (such as zoo experts), books, and Web sites. Students should discuss with the class the information they have obtained so far. Information should be recorded in their storyboard journal. Pictures can be drawn in the journal and/or collected from Internet.

Refer back to the Essential Question. Have students take a few minutes to discuss their ideas together and record them on the tablet PC (with a projector display) or on the whiteboard. Bring the discussion back to the whole group and add ideas to the Essential Question document created at the beginning of the unit.

Have students get out their K-W-L chart to fill in the "Learn" section with what they have learned so far. Have them revisit their questions in the Wonder section to see if they have been answered yet. Have volunteers share some of their own responses to add to the class K-W-L chart. Encourage students to continue answering the Essential Question by adding responses to the Essential Question document in front of the class.

Week Three. Graph data and information using the interactive whiteboard. Give students pertinent data to graph. Using the tablet PC and projector or whiteboard and graphing software, have students take turns adding information about their animal. For example, present characteristics of various chosen animals on the graph. The first characteristic will be weight. Student will collect data about the animals and then create a weight bar graph showing which animal is the heaviest and which is the lightest. Microsoft Excel is useful for graphing data, and both Excel spreadsheets and Excel-generated charts and graphs allow inked annotations when run on the tablet PC. Demonstrate various types of graphs with students, comparing and contrasting various characteristics. Have students choose a graph they would like to include in their final presentation.

Week Four. Reintroduce and answer the Unit and Content Questions. Students demonstrate their understanding of these questions by first completing research on a particular species and then summarizing the information in a storyboard journal, which will later be turned into a multimedia demonstration. Show students the rubric that will be used to assess their final project. Demonstrate how the rubric will be used, and give them a checklist they should use to create the project.

Using the information obtained through the research, have students color North American maps, showing where the various species live. This picture will be scanned into the final project (or, use ArtRage on the tablet PC).

Endangered Animals. Did anyone choose an endangered animal? Think about a world without this animal. Who or what will be impacted? Guide students through these higher-order questions and generate other questions based on student responses and interests. Explore other opportunities to research and present on this topic.

Concluding Activities. Students will participate in an Activote quiz (or similar) over basic needs of animals and the general characteristics. A spiral review of social studies content and math concepts will be included. In addition, vocabulary words will be reviewed and assessed.

Students will work together to create a multimedia PowerPoint presentation of a North American animal. They will use the data and information collected along the way to create the presentation. Students will have a choice to work collaboratively or independently on the project. When the projects are completed, the students will have a celebration presentation to share their expertise on their animal(s). Students will also have the flexibility to create a physical model or draw a picture of their animal to include in the presentation.

Assessment

Project impact will be measured through a variety of rubrics, checklists, surveys, observations, and assessments. Rubrics will be used for their digital journals and multimedia projects. Assessments will also be conducted through the use of Promethean Activote (or similar software) and teacher-created pre- and post-assessments. The students will self-monitor through conferences with teachers, peers, and also by completing self-evaluations. Student surveys will be completed to provide feedback on their thoughts of the project. Finally, teachers will observe student collaboration, research skills, and student work. Ultimately, the impact of this project will be illustrated in the students' presentation of their digital portfolios.

Adaptations

Resource Student

- Make modifications as dictated in the student's IEP.

- Have struggling students pair with another student for projects.

- Provide resource students with appropriate text (with various pictures and captions). In addition, provide students with audio books and Internet aides.

- Allow student to choose presentation method.

Gifted Student

- Encourage broad and deep research.

- Have students make additional comparisons, such as interdependence and conservation.

- Have students research how endangered species and extinct species affect their ecosystem; and, in turn, how these changes in ecosystems affect humans.

English Language Learner

- Encourage support from first-language speakers who are more proficient in English.

- Provide extra time for completing the assignments.

- Offer teacher-created templates and graphic organizers for students to fill in.

- Use visuals, manipulative learning tools, and illustrated text.

National Educational Technology Standards for Students

1.a, b; 2.a, b, d; 3.b, d; 4.b; 5.b; 6.a, b

"Brrr, It's Alive"

ENGLISH LANGUAGE ARTS • GRADES K–2

Description

Guessing riddles is something primary-grade students always enjoy. The creation of riddles requires children to think analytically about what they are describing in order to provide enough information to distinguish it from other similar things.

In this activity, students write a riddle that gives clues about an animal. Other students try to guess the animal's identity. The information gathered to create the riddle forms the foundation for writing a report about cold-weather animals. Students learn to organize information they have found about a cold-weather animal and then add details and place their information in an outline. Students then create text and an illustration, or they can scan an image that correlates with the text.

The project culminates with a combined project—an electronic presentation—that includes all of the students' information. Because this activity focuses on the effective use of language, be sure to provide additional resources and media that will aid comprehension for students whose first language is not English.

Objectives

Students will:

- use oral, written, and visual language (for different purposes) to communicate effectively with a variety of audiences.

- use a variety of technological resources to gather and synthesize information.

- use a variety of technological resources to create and communicate knowledge.

- read a range of print materials to build an understanding of texts and acquire new information.

- write in two forms: riddle and report.

Materials

- Tablet PCs

- Digital projector

- Scanner

- Tablet PC software for:

    - Journals and note taking (e.g., Microsoft Journal or OneNote)

    - Concept-mapping (e.g., Inspiration or Kidspiration)

    - Drawing (e.g., Ambient Design's ArtRage)

    - Presentations (e.g., Microsoft PowerPoint)

Preparation and Planning

- Consult the library media specialist for available resources. Select magazines, books, Web sites, etc.

- Demonstrate to students how concept–mapping software works.

- Schedule time to confer with students, individually or in small groups, about their animal choices.

- To facilitate students' construction of outlines and electronic writing with the tablet PC, consider scheduling extra volunteers in the classroom for those days.

- Demonstrate scanning and drawing software.

- Consider combining all of the projects into a single electronic format to facilitate sharing and dissemination.

Procedures

1. As part of students' Know-Wonder-Learn (K-W-L) charts, have students brainstorm what they already know about animals that live in cold-weather climates and what more they want to learn. Stimulate discussion about what the term *cold* means. Provide students with a short introduction to resources they can use to acquire information. Encourage them to browse through selected materials—nonfiction books, instructional television programs, appropriate Web sites, and the like.

2. Make sure that enough types of cold-weather animals are listed with information sources so that each student can select one for the study. From selected resources, have students gather materials they can use.

3. In table groups, have students share a) what they have learned so far about their animals; b) how they are classifying the animals (e.g., by specific cold-weather climates); and c) how they can help share resources they come across for animals being studied by other members of the table group.

4. Review the parts of a riddle, what makes one interesting, and what constitutes a good question. Provide examples of good riddles. Have students use their tablet PCs to write a riddle about the animals they have chosen.

5. Have students use their tablet PCs and drawing software (such as ArtRage) to illustrate their animals in a way that does not give away the animal's identity. Provide an example for students to get them started.

6. Have students read their riddles aloud and have other students guess the animal. Use their drawings for additional clues.

7. The riddles should demonstrate what kinds of facts students can gather about their animals. As the riddles are read, make a list of these facts. The class can then brainstorm common attributes for cold-weather animals. While using concept-mapping software to make an outline or a map of the common attributes, students check to see which attributes are true for all their animals.

8. Students choose four attributes to use for their own reports. They find at least three details for each topic they have chosen, and they add that information to the outline/map.

9. Students work from the outline/map to write a report or story in PowerPoint for class distribution.

10. Projects (riddle and story or report) can be shared by posting them on the school or class Web site, or by creating hard copies.

Assessment

- For concept-mapping activities, provide each student with a checklist for the teacher to sign.

- Assess the writing of the report for content, accuracy, and mechanics. Create a dual scoring rubric that is consistent with current student levels.

- Have students help create and modify a rubric for assessing electronic information, including text content, graphics, illustrations, and creativity; use a scale of excellent, good, fair, and poor.

Adaptations

This activity can be adapted for a whole class using one animal, as well as with students working in cooperative or collaborative groups. Younger students can dramatize an animal by taking a digital photo of another student imitating the animal.

National Educational Technology Standards for Students

1.a, b; 2.a, b; 3.b; 5.b; 6.a, b

Exploring Wetlands

SCIENCE • GRADES 3–5

Description

In this unit, students watch videos of marsh and wetland areas, find these areas on maps, and locate these areas on Google Earth. Students also research a wetland animal and create a riddle about the animal in PowerPoint. These riddles are then posted to the school's wetlands Web site for other students to read. The procedure specifies local wetlands, but any wetlands area can be used in this lesson.

Objectives

Students will:

- learn about animal/plant adaptations in various environments and explore ways that organisms protect themselves.

- identify and locate local wetland areas and explain their value.

- identify and describe animals that live in these habitats.

- create a riddle about a wetland animal and make a PowerPoint presentation to illustrate their riddle.

Materials

- Tablet PCs

- Digital projector

- Internet access

- Google Earth application (http://earth.google.com)

- Streaming video of local marshes and wetlands (optional)

- Web sites of wetlands (local wetlands, if available) for a map, and pictures of wetland areas and animals

- Riddle Web sites:

  - National Institute of Environmental Health Services (NIEHS) Kids' Pages riddles: http://kids.niehs.nih.gov/rd1.htm

  - Increase Brain Power's "What Am I?" riddles: www.increasebrainpower.com/what-am-i-riddles.html

- Tablet PC software for:

  - Concept-mapping (e.g., Inspiration or Kidspiration)

  - Presentations (e.g., Microsoft PowerPoint)

  - Word processing (e.g., Microsoft Word)

Procedures

1. Introduce students to marshes by watching a streaming video about marshes and wetlands.

2. Using the tablet PC and projector, help students locate local marshes and other wetland areas using specialized research maps. These maps should show all types of wetland areas in the respective area, as well as their geographical relation to the school's location.

3. Help students use Google Earth to see what these areas look like in an aerial view. Students can use the pen feature on the tablet PC to mark different types of wetland areas.

4. After locating different marshes and wetland areas, have students look at pictures of these areas using locally-produced area wetlands Web sites (if available).

5. Lead a discussion of riddles with students. Have students give examples of riddles and look at examples of riddles on the Internet. This exercise prepares them to write riddles about animals that live in the respective marsh and wetlands.

6. Give students time to look at the respective wetland Web sites to learn about animals that live there. Their assignment is to choose a wetland animal, do research on it, and use the facts they find to create a riddle about that animal.

7. In the Inspiration program, help students make a diagram with their animal's name in the center and (coming from the center) facts that will become clues for their riddle. The result is a diagram that students will follow to create a riddle.

8. Have students use the tablet PCs and PowerPoint to create single slides with their riddle clues. The second-to-last slide in the sequence says, "What Am I?" On the final slide, students draw or paste in a picture of the animal and the name of the animal. Help students to animate the slide show so that the clues come in one by one, with the animal's picture and its name coming last. Students may also format the background with a picture of the animal's environment.

9. Have students present these PowerPoint presentations to the class. These PowerPoint presentations can also be posted to the school's Web site and/or burned on a CD to be shared with other classes in the school.

Assessment

- Quizzes will be given on streaming videos and maps viewed.

- PowerPoint presentations will be graded using teacher-made rubrics.

National Educational Technology Standards for Students

1.b; 3.b, c; 4.a; 6.a, b

Fairytales: Compare and Contrast

ENGLISH LANGUAGE ARTS • GRADES 3–5

Description

In a teacher-led demonstration, students will differentiate story aspects of two versions of "Hansel and Gretel," told from two different points of view. Independently, students will read similar stories and compare and contrast fairytale characteristics.

Objective

Students will:

- identify story elements that are the same and different in similar fairytale stories. After a whole class lesson and practice, students will be able to use concept-mapping software to fill in their own Venn diagram to compare and contrast a new pair of similar fairytales.

Materials

- Tablet PCs

- Digital projector

- Printer (optional)

- Grimm Brothers' version of "Hansel and Gretel" and an alternate version, such as *The Diary of Hansel and Gretel* (Moerbeek, 2002)

- Traditional version of "The Three Little Pigs" and an alternate version, such as *The True Story of the 3 Little Pigs* (Scieszka & Smith, 1989)

- Teacher-created template of Venn diagram (for the comparison of two stories), created using Kidspiration; or paper copy of the Venn diagram template (optional)

- Tablet PC software for:
  - Journals and note taking (e.g., Microsoft Journal or OneNote)
  - Word processing (e.g., Microsoft Word)
  - Concept-mapping (Kidspiration)

Procedures

Introduction

1. Review characteristics of fairytales using Kidspiration bubble graphic organizer.

Activity

2. Read the classic Grimm Brothers' version of "Hansel and Gretel," and then read *The Diary of Hansel and Gretel*.

3. Display a pre-designed Kidspiration Venn diagram.

4. Begin brainstorming similarities of the two versions. Create entries into the Venn diagram describing the entry procedure for each entry. There will be many entries, and using different colors for each entry type helps students distinguish them. A tablet PC's inking capability makes this easy.

5. Invite students to make entries (with teacher assistance or instruction) on the tablet PC as they volunteer the information.

6. Continue with the differences of the stories, expanding the area of the circles, as needed.

Conclusion

7. Read aloud both a traditional version of "The Three Little Pigs" and *The Real Story of the 3 Little Pigs* (from the wolf's point of view).

8. If tablet PCs are deployed one-to-one, have students bring up your pre-designed Kidspiration Venn diagram; otherwise, hand out paper copies of the diagram. Direct students to write down their contrasts and comparisons, using different ink colors to help organize them.

Assessment

Students use their Venn diagram to compare and contrast similar fairytales. If their diagram is completed on paper, they transfer the information to Kidspiration software.

Rubric: Compare and Contrast

Beginning. Student either compares or contrasts similar fairytales on paper.

Developing. Student both compares and contrasts similar fairytales on paper.

Accomplished. Student both compares and contrasts similar fairytales for three story aspects on paper.

Exemplary. Student both compares and contrasts similar fairytales for three story aspects, and transfers the information to their 2-circle Venn diagram.

Rubric: Compare and Contrast Using 2-Circle Venn Diagram

Beginning. Student is able to identify three story aspects that are the same for both fairytales and three story aspects that are different for each fairytale on a two-circle Venn diagram.

Developing. Student is able to identify at least five story aspects that are the same for both fairytales and at least five story aspects that are different for each fairytale on a two-circle Venn diagram.

Accomplished. Student is able to identify five or more story aspects that are the same for both fairytales and five or more story aspects that are different for each fairytale on a two-circle Venn diagram, and then (if done on a paper diagram) transfer that information (*with assistance*) to a pre-designed Venn diagram generated by Kidspiration software.

Exemplary. Student is able to identify eight or more story aspects that are the same for both fairytales and eight or more story aspects that are different for each fairytale on a two-circle Venn diagram, and then (if done on paper) transfer that information (*independently*) to a pre-designed Venn diagram generated by Kidspiration software.

National Educational Technology Standards for Students

2.a, 6.a

The Scientific Method

SCIENCE • GRADES 6–8

Description

The purpose of this learning experience is to build on students' listening, speaking, reading, and writing abilities for critical analysis and evaluation through mathematical analysis and scientific inquiry. By studying the scientific method, students will go through the process of developing a hypothesis, performing an experiment, showing findings, and analyzing results.

Objectives

Students will:

- learn the steps of the scientific method.
- learn that changing a variable affects the outcome of the experiment.
- chart and graph data.
- interpret and analyze results.

Materials

- Tablet PCs
- Digital projector
- Internet access
- Tablet PC software for:
  - Journals and note taking (e.g., Microsoft Journal or OneNote)
  - Presentations (e.g., Microsoft PowerPoint)
  - Illustrating physics concepts and shapes (e.g., Physics Illustrator; optional)

Procedures

1. Review the scientific method with students. For an online graphic, see "Steps of the Scientific Method" at: http://home.att.net/~teaching/science/method.pdf

2. Introduce examples of the scientific method in action, using sites such as BBC's KS2 Bitesize Revision–Science at: www.bbc.co.uk/schools/ks2bitesize/science/

3. Using visual elements such as illustrations, simulations, photographs, videos, charts, graphs, symbols, diagrams, and tables, illustrate an area of scientific study. For example, an area of inquiry might be gradient, and how slope and weight affect the distance an object travels. **Note:** Physics Illustrator on the tablet PC is a great tool for physics problems.

4. Using the tablet PC and projector, demonstrate how to conduct an experiment using the scientific method (this experiment can be performed online via a site like KS2 or by using Physics Illustrator). This demonstration includes showing students how to conduct an experiment, record the data, and present results.

5. During the demonstration, make it clear to students that:

   • In a controlled experiment, the independent variable (the variable that is changed during the experiment) affects the dependent variable (the variable that changes in response to the changes of the independent variable). There must also be controlled or constant variables; otherwise the data may be skewed or invalid.

   • The purpose of an experiment is to test (prove or disprove) a hypothesis.

   • An experiment shows a cause and effect relationship in nature: Changes in one thing can cause a predictable change in another.

6. Direct students to visit a site (or sites) like KS2.

7. Demonstrate Physics Illustrator.

8. Help students develop hypotheses as they go through an experiment. Students should address the key question that was modeled for them in the demonstration; in this case: How will slope and weight affect the distance traveled by an object?

9. Direct students to conduct an experiment and record their data by using their tablet PCs and making notes of their findings with Microsoft Journal or OneNote.

10. Have students show and analyze their findings and results through data and charts, and then summarize their findings to the rest of the class through a PowerPoint presentation.

Assessment

PowerPoint presentations are used to assess how students have organized, analyzed, and evaluated their findings and ideas. Students' conclusions measure whether they have been able to defend or refute their original hypotheses. They also provide an opportunity for students to share their ideas orally with visual cues.

National Educational Technology Standards for Students

1.c; 2.b; 3.a, c, d; 4.a, b, c; 5.b; 6.a, b

Birthstone Project

ENGLISH LANGUAGE ARTS, SCIENCE • GRADES 6–8

Description

This lesson sequence is designed to be an interdisciplinary project for students taking both English language arts and earth sciences. In groups, students learn about minerals in general, and their birthstone in particular, through online research, writing, and recording an oral narrative.

Objectives

English language arts, earth sciences, and technology come together in a meaningful way through research, writing, and oral recording about birthstones. Students will:

- focus on planning and pacing to build their study skills and collaborate effectively within groups and across two classes.

- gather, interpret, and present information about the formation, identification, classification, and use of minerals in the context of an earth sciences research paper.

- gather, interpret, and present information about their personal birthstone and pertinent historical events in a recorded English language arts narrative.

Materials

- Tablet PCs
- Digital projector (optional)
- Digital camera (optional)
- Tablet PC software for:
  - Note taking (e.g., Microsoft Journal or OneNote)
  - Word processing (e.g., Microsoft Word)

- Collaboration (e.g., DyKnow Vision or a blogging utility)

- Multimedia recording (e.g., Adobe Premiere Pro, Audacity)

Preparation and Planning

- Assign students to groups according to birthstone. If the same class of students takes both earth sciences and English language arts, then the groups will remain the same in both classes. If not, the groups will differ in each class.

- Create a research outline to distribute to students in earth sciences class. This outline should help them discover and record information about the formation, identification, classification, and uses of a teacher-created list of minerals. The outline should contain a section for recording in-depth information about a particular birthstone.

- Create a research outline to distribute to students in English language arts class. This outline should help them discover and record information about historical events from the month and year they were born, as well as information about the significance and perceived or symbolic qualities of a particular birthstone.

- Develop a timeline for students to use to keep track of deadlines. These projects may generally be completed in two weeks.

- Use a collaboration application (e.g., DyKnow Vision) or a course blog to distribute this timeline to students and parents with all project deadlines clearly noted. All students should cross-reference their research assignments and deadlines in their personal planners.

- Have students create a traveling folder on their tablet PCs entitled "Birthstone Project." This simple strategy cuts down on "I lost my research" excuses, as student groups work on this project in two separate classes.

- At the project's midpoint, provide a notification to parents via the course blog, and in both classes have each student group report their progress.

Procedures: Earth Sciences

1. Have books, charts, periodicals, and a pre-screened list of Web sites available in the classroom. Students research the formation, identification, classification, and use of minerals, and identify their birthstone's characteristics and use in the context of earth sciences.

2. Direct students to fill in their research outlines for a research paper to be created later. The research paper will include multimedia elements. Following a research outline helps students learn basic research and recording skills. As part of the research phase, emphasize taking notes for a bibliography.

3. Have students gather appropriate mineral images and even video to include in their research papers.

Procedures: English Language Arts

1. Have books, charts, periodicals, and a pre-screened list of Web sites available in the classroom so student groups may discover and record significant historical events during or close to the group's birth month and year.

2. Next, have the group research and record the historical significance and perceived or symbolic qualities of the group's birthstone.

3. Student groups will now write a narrative essay titled "What Happened When We Were Born." The essay should start with an exploration of the birthstone and its historical significance and perceived or symbolic qualities; then the essay should explore selected historical events that tie in to those qualities. (For example, garnet symbolizes perseverance. Students would attempt to find a historical event from their birth month that demonstrates this quality.)

4. Student groups will record their essays in their own voices. Each group member should record part of the essay.

Procedures: Technology Integration

1. Have students use pre-screened Web sites to research minerals, birthstones, and historical events. They should develop a file of scanned or downloaded images and use a digital camera to take their own images of common

minerals. Introduce and explain the concepts of copyright and intellectual property when directing students to download images from the Internet.

2. Using their tablet PCs, students may write on their blank research outlines; then, using handwriting-recognition software, convert handwritten information from their research outlines into typed text.

3. Using their tablet PCs to collaborate, student groups expand their outlines into paragraphs. The earth sciences project becomes a research paper with multimedia elements, and the English language arts project becomes an oral recording.

4. Teach advanced word processing skills so that student groups can include a title page, table of contents, page numbers, bibliographic information, and image placement in their research papers.

5. Teach students to use recording and editing software such as Audacity or Adobe Premiere Pro for their oral recording.

Extension

- Create a birthstone Web site that will be a repository for student research papers and oral recordings, grouped by birthstone. Include multimedia elements.

- Host a technology night where students present their contributions to the birthstone Web site.

Assessment

Develop a grading rubric in earth sciences, English language arts, and technology that reflects each discipline's emphasis. Distribute and explain these rubrics in both classes.

National Educational Technology Standards for Students

1.a, b; 2.b; 3.b, c; 4.a, b; 5.b; 6.a, b

Habitat Investigation

SCIENCE • GRADES 9–12

Description

Students use the Mission Creek Web site and Mission Creek Guided Tour lesson plan to learn about a natural habitat, including the geology, topography, plants, animals, and human activities integrated within this habitat. Alternately, students use a teacher-created Web site that describes a natural habitat in their own community.

Objective

Students will:

- learn valuable information about a natural habitat by using worksheets designed especially for this activity.

Materials

- Tablet PCs
- Digital projector
- Internet access
- Tablet PC software for:
  - Journals and note taking (e.g., Microsoft Journal or OneNote)
- Mission Creek Web site:
  www.msnucleus.org/watersheds/mission/missioncreek.html
- Mission Creek Guided Tour lesson plan worksheets
  (www.msnucleus.org/watersheds/mission/GuildedTour.html)

Procedures

1. Use the Mission Creek Guided Tour lesson plan material for this lesson. You may instead want to create your own Web site that describes a natural habitat in your community. This could be done as part of a teaching team, possibly with the help of local community organizations.

2. Using the tablet PC and projector, introduce the lesson and activity by showing students this Web site. Show students how to navigate through the Web site, such that they will be able to gather the information they need to complete their habitat investigation worksheets.

3. Using a brainstorming session and OneNote, suggest to students some possible types of living organisms that may be found at the habitat. Then, lead students in a discussion about the importance of preserving our environment and the role humans play in that preservation. Use the OneNote materials for a post-activity discussion.

4. After the discussion, divide students into groups of four or five to begin work on their habitat worksheets in class.

5. Have students complete the worksheets. This activity can be finished in class over several class periods, or students can take the activity home and finish it there (if they have computers and Internet access at home). Whether work should be completed in class or at home should be decided before beginning the activity. This way, some students don't finish at home when it should be done in class.

6. Using the tablet PC and projector, access the habitat Web site and take students through the worksheets, discussing each of the entries. Engage students in a discussion—using OneNote entries from the pre-activity discussion—to compare and contrast their findings.

Assessment

Review the completed worksheets to determine students' ability to understand and interpret the materials presented.

National Educational Technology Standards for Students

2.a; 4.a, b; 5.b; 6.a

Lining Up Data

MATHEMATICS • GRADES 9–12

Description

Students make informed predictions based on such real-world data as phone bills, postage rates, and airline schedules. Students use the tablet PC to plot data and draw lines that fit the data they have graphed. They then use these lines to make predictions that extrapolate or interpolate the data. Students conduct research to find other appropriate data sets, develop questions, and answer questions developed by other students.

Objectives

Students will:

- examine the concept of functions (including graphs, domain, and range of interest) using real-world data.

- make models of data and predictions based on that data.

- discuss and defend their conclusions with other students.

- use a variety of resources to gather information.

- show that math can be used to synthesize data.

Materials

- Tablet PCs

- Digital projector

- Tablet PC software for:

    - Dynamically drawing curves and surfaces (Summa's Winplot)

    - An on-screen calculator (optional)

    - A mathematical sketch-recognition system (FluidMath)

    - Visualization of mathematical concepts (Geometer's Sketchpad)

Procedures

1. Find appropriate introductory linear data sets and ask students to interpret them. For example, identify a long-distance phone bill with several calls to the same number, and then record the length of the calls in minutes and the charge for each call.

2. Use the selected data set to demonstrate how data and graphing are connected. Have students plot data on the tablet PC and choose appropriate "window ranges" to display the data. In this example, the length of the call is plotted along the x-axis and the cost along the y-axis.

3. With the students, develop a mathematical model to fit the data, writing it in functional form. Graphically, the data looks like a straight line, with every minute "costing" a certain amount of money. The connection between the algebraic and graphical representations of straight lines may be elicited here.

4. Have students calculate the parameters of the model using the data, and display the model graphically along with the data. Students will derive ideas such as "Since 5 minutes cost $2, each minute costs $0.40." Students learn to identify the meaning of their parameters, as in "slope is the cost/minute" or "the y-intercept is the connect charge."

5. Help students judge the model's "line of best fit" and adjust the model as necessary. By looking at their graphs, students can see how closely their model line comes to the data points. In addition, during the adjustments of their connection charges and costs per minute, students can come to understand the different effects in each of the graph's parameters.

6. Direct students to compare their fit with those of other students. Have them discuss and defend their models and parameters, as well as develop a measure for the closeness of the fit. Students will compare graphs and generally work toward deciding which graph is a better model of the data.

7. Group students for an independent project that focuses on data sets and lines of best fit. Have students find other data sets from other sources such as the library or Internet. Using the data sets, follow the same procedure as in the previous activities. Have students develop questions based on these data sets, and have them exchange both data sets and questions with other students. Linear data sets can be found for almost anything—for example, for house prices per square foot; for minutes played versus points scored for sports players; for postage rates versus weight; and for airplane flight time versus miles flown.

Assessment

At minimum, evaluate students on their ability to:

- plot data correctly.

- calculate lines of fit and to explain the significance of the parameters in their equation.

- explain and defend their choice of fit to other students.

Develop a rubric with students for scoring the independent projects. This rubric should align with the learning-activity objectives. Students should be aware of and understand the scoring rubric at the beginning of the project. As the project progresses, students can help refine the various levels of the rubric.

Comments

A first data set that works well is a phone bill from a calling card (e.g., someone calling home from a conference). Having an entry for a single minute is helpful, because it is sometimes presumed that whatever the charge for the first minute is the charge for every minute, and good discussions can ensue from this presumption. Generally, this activity is used without ever mentioning "slope" or "intercept." Wait until students are proficient at their calculations and interpretations before introducing this vocabulary.

Extension

Use Geometer's Sketchpad to graphically show the meaning of "least-squares error."

National Educational Technology Standards for Students

1.c, d; 2.a, d; 3.d; 4.a, c; 5.b; 6.a, b

A | Bibliography

Alvarado, C. (2004). Sketch recognition user interfaces: Guidelines for design and development. In R. Davis, J. Landay, T. Stahovich, R. Miller, E. Saund (Eds.), *Making Pen-Based Interaction Intelligent and Natural: Papers from the 2004 Fall Symposium* (pp. 8–14). Technical Report FS-04-06. Menlo Park, CA: American Association for Artificial Intelligence.

Alvarado, C. & Davis, R. (2004). SketchREAD: a multi-domain sketch recognition engine. In *UIST '04: Proceedings of the 17th Annual ACM Symposium on User Interface Software and Technology* (pp. 23–32). New York: ACM Press.

Anderson, R. J., Hoyer, C., Wolfman, S. A., & Anderson, R. (2004). A study of digital ink in lecture presentation. In *CHI '04: Proceedings of the SIGCHI Conference on Human Factors in Computing Systems* (pp. 567–574). New York: ACM Press.

Brown, David G. (Ed.). (2003). *Ubiquitous computing: The universal use of computers on college campuses*. Williston, VT: Anker Publishing.

Calhoun, C., Stahovich, T.F., Kurtoglu, T., & Kara, L.B. (2002). Recognizing multi-stroke symbols. In *AAAI Spring Symposium on Sketch Understanding* (pp. 15–23). Technical Report SS-02-08. Menlo Park, CA: AAAI Press.

Carryer, J. E. (2006). The tablet PC as a platform for screencasting lectures. In D. Berque, J. Prey, R. Reed (Eds.). *The impact of tablet PCs and pen-based technology on education* (pp. 41–48). West Lafayette, IN: Purdue University Press.

Cicchino, R., & Mirliss, D. (2004). Tablet PCs: A powerful teaching tool. In G. Richards (Ed.). *Proceedings of World Conference on E-Learning in Corporate, Government, Healthcare, and Higher Education, 2004* (pp. 543–548). Chesapeake, VA: AACE.

Crocker, W. (2006). *Using a tablet PC as a staging tool.* Retrieved June 1, 2007, from http://wickedstageact2.typepad.com/life_on_the_wicked_stage_/2006/03/using_a_tablet_.html

Derting, T., & Cox, R. (2007). *A campus-wide initiative to develop, deploy, and assess five models of technology-enhanced teaching and learning.* Retrieved October 31, 2007, from www.cfkeep.org/html/snapshot.php?id=59947744253974

Donovan, L., Hartley, K., & Strudler, N. (2007). Teacher concerns during initial implementation of a one-to-one laptop initiative at the middle school level. *Journal of Research on Technology in Education, 39*(3), 263–286.

Foley, J. D., van Dam, A., Feiner, S. K., & Hughes, J. F. (1993). *Introduction to computer graphics.* Reading, MA: Addison-Wesley.

Forsberg, A.S., Dieterich, M. K., & Zeleznik, R.C. (1998). The music notepad. In *Proceedings of the 11th Annual ACM Symposium on User interface Software and Technology* (pp. 203–210). New York: ACM Press.

Friedman, T. L. (2006). *The world is flat.* (First revision and expanded ed.). New York: Farrar, Straus, & Giroux.

Glover, D., Miller, D., Averis, D., & Door, V. (2005). Leadership implications of using interactive whiteboards: Linking technology and pedagogy in the management of change. *Management in Education, 18*(5), 27–30.

Hammond, T. & Davis, R. (2002). Tahuti: A geometrical sketch recognition system for UMLl class diagrams. In *AAAI Spring Symposium on Sketch Understanding* (pp. 59-68). Stanford, CA: AAAI Press.

Hammond, T. (2007). LADDER: A perceptually based language to simplify sketch recognition user interface development. PhD thesis. Massachusetts Institute of Technology. Available from http://rationale.csail.mit.edu/publications/Hammond2007Ladder.pdf

Hammond, T. (2007a). *Sketch recognition at Texas A&M University.* Available from http://faculty.cs.tamu.edu/hammond/publications/2007HammondBrownPenCentric.pdf

Hse, H., & Newton, A.R. (2004). Recognition and beautification of multi-stroke symbols in digital ink. In R. Davis, J. Landay, T. Stahovich, R. Miller, E. Saund (Eds.), *Making Pen-Based Interaction Intelligent and Natural: Papers from the 2004 Fall Symposium* (pp. 78-84). Technical Report FS-04-06. Menlo Park, CA: American Association for Artificial Intelligence..

Hulls, C. C. W. (2005). Using a tablet PC for classroom instruction. In *Proceedings of the 35th ASEE/IEEE Frontiers in Education Conference*, Indianapolis, IN. Available from www.cte.uwaterloo.ca/research/TBRG/presentations_publications/hullsieee.pdf

Koile, K., & Singer, D. (2006). Development of a tablet PC-based system to increase instructor-student classroom interactions and student learning. In D. Berque, J. Prey, R. Reed (Eds.). *The impact of tablet PCs and pen-based technology on education: Vignettes, evaluations, and future directions* (pp. 115–122). West Lafayette, IN: Purdue University Press.

LaViola, J., & Zeleznik, R. (2004, August). MathPad2: A system for the creation and exploration of mathematical sketches. ACM transactions on graphics. *Proceedings of SIGGRAPH, 23*(3), 432–440.

Leeds, K. (2006). *Technology: Fad or fixture? A study on students' perceptions of using tablet PCs during class.* Retrieved May 4, 2007, from www.cccone.org/scholars/05-06/KelvinLeedsMonograph.pdf

Merriam-Webster's Dictionary and Thesaurus (11th ed.) (2006). Springfield, MA: Merriam-Webster.

Meyer, A. (1995, July). Pen computing: A technology overview and a vision. *SIGCHI Bull, 27*(3), 46–90.

Mock, K. (2004). Teaching with tablet PCs. *Journal of Computing in Small Colleges, 20*(2), 17–27.

Mock, K. (2007). *Tablet PC collaborative software development for fieldwork-based courses.* HP Technology for Teaching report. Retrieved June 1, 2007, from www.cfkeep.org/html/snapshot.php?id=70139735071119

Motion Computing. (2007). *C5 mobile clinical assistant.* Retrieved April 29, 2007, from www.motioncomputing.com/products/tablet_pc_c5.asp

Payton, M. (2006). Evaluation of the deployment of GoBinder on tablet PCs as an aid to student note-taking and organization. In D. Berque, J. Prey, R. Reed (Eds.). *The impact of tablet PCs and pen-based technology on education: Vignettes, evaluations, and future directions* (pp. 139–148). West Lafayette, IN: Purdue University Press.

Penuel, William R. (2006). Implementation and effects of one-to-one computing initiatives: A research synthesis. *Journal of Research on Technology in Education 38*(3), 329–348.

Petty, D., & Gunawardena A. (2007). The use of tablet PCs in early mathematics education. In J. Prey, R. Reed, D. Berque (Eds.), *The impact of tablet PCs and pen-based technology on education: Beyond the tipping point* (pp. 89–96). West Lafayette, IN: Purdue University Press.

Saund, E., Fleet, D., Larner, D., & Mahoney, J. (2003). Perceptually-supported image editing of text and graphics. In *UIST '03: Proceedings of the 16th Annual ACM Symposium on User Interface Software and Technology* (pp. 183–192). New York: ACM Press..

Schroeder, D. (2004, November). Tablet PCs and collaboration software improve classroom engagement at Cabrillo High School. *T.H.E. Journal.* Retrieved June 4, 2007, from www.thejournal.com/articles/17040

Sezgin, T.M., Stahovich, T., & Davis, R. (2001). Sketch-based interfaces: Early processing for sketch understanding. In *Proceedings from the 2001 Workshop on Perceptive User Interfaces* (pp. 1–8). New York: ACM Press.

Sloan, K., & Borse, J. (2006). A case study of pen-enabled technology in a sixth-grade math classroom. In D. Berque, J. Prey, R. Reed (Eds.), *The impact of tablet PCs and pen-based technology on education: Vignettes, evaluations, and future directions* (pp. 115–122). West Lafayette, IN: Purdue University Press.

SMART Technologies. (2006). *Interactive whiteboards and learning: Improving student learning outcomes and streamlining lesson planning.* Available from www2.smarttech. com/NR/rdonlyres/2C729F6E-0A8D-42B8-9B32-F90BE0A746D8/0/Int_Whiteboard_Research_Whitepaper_Update.pdf

Sommerich, C., & Collura, K. (2007). Learning with mobile technology in high school: A human factors perspective. In J. Prey, R. Reed, D. Berque (Eds.), *The impact of tablet PCs and pen-based technology on education: Beyond the tipping point* (pp. 127–136). West Lafayette, IN: Purdue University Press.

Stahovich, T.F. (1997). Interpreting the engineer's sketch: A picture is worth a thousand constraints. In *Reasoning with Diagrammatic Representations II: Papers from the AAAI Fall Symposium* (pp. 31–38). Technical Report FS-97-03. Menlo Park, CA: AAAI Press.

Student Life Studies. (2007). *What we know about A&M undergraduates: Technology.* College Station: Texas A&M University.

Sutherland, I. B. (1963). Sketchpad, a man-machine graphical communication system. In *Proceedings of the Spring Joint Computer Conference* (pp. 329–346). Electronic version with new preface available from www.cl.cam.ac.uk/techreports/UCAM-CL-TR-574.pdf

TabletPCReview. (2007). *Tablet PC database.* Retrieved April 29, 2007, from www.tabletpcreview.com/price/

Tan, E. (2007, April 19). Intel readies chip for mobile computing. *Business Week.* Available from www.businessweek.com/globalbiz/content/apr2007/gb20070419_847785.htm?chan=top+news_top+news+index_global+business

Teaching, Learning, & Technology in Higher Education. (2007). *One tablet classrooms @ Murray State University*. Retrieved October 31, 2007, from http://h20325.www2.hp.com/blogs/highered/archive/2006/07/28/1399.html

Tenneson, L., & Becker, S. (2005). ChemPad: Generating 3D molecules from 2D sketches. In *SIGGRAPH '05: ACM SIGGRAPH 2005 Posters* (p. 87). New York: ACM Press.

Thompson, S. (2006). LABTOP: The tablet PC at the center of learning. HP Technology for Teaching report, Retrieved June 1, 2007, from www.csmate.colostate.edu/labtop/hpreport.html

Warschauer, M. (2006). *Going one-to-one. Educational Leadership, 63*(4), 34–38, Alexandria, VA: Association for Supervision and Curriculum Development (ERIC Document reproduction Service No. EJ745473).

Yu, B., & Cai, S. (2003). A domain-independent system for sketch recognition. In *Proceedings of the 1st International Conference on Computer Graphics and Interactive Techniques in Australasia and Southeast Asia* (pp. 141–147). New York: ACM Press.

Zucker, A. (2004). Developing a research agenda for ubiquitous computing in schools. *J. Educational Computing Research, 30*(4), 371–386.

B | National Educational Technology Standards

National Educational Technology Standards for Students (NETS•S)

The National Educational Technology Standards for students are divided into six broad categories. Standards within each category are to be introduced, reinforced, and mastered by students. Teachers can use these standards as guidelines for planning technology-based activities in which students achieve success in learning, communication, and life skills.

1. **Creativity and Innovation**

    Students demonstrate creative thinking, construct knowledge, and develop innovative products and processes using technology. Students:

    a. apply existing knowledge to generate new ideas, products, or processes

    b. create original works as a means of personal or group expression

    c. use models and simulations to explore complex systems and issues

    d. identify trends and forecast possibilities

2. **Communication and Collaboration**

   Students use digital media and environments to communicate and work collaboratively, including at a distance, to support individual learning and contribute to the learning of others. Students:

   a. interact, collaborate, and publish with peers, experts, or others employing a variety of digital environments and media

   b. communicate information and ideas effectively to multiple audiences using a variety of media and formats

   c. develop cultural understanding and global awareness by engaging with learners of other cultures

   d. contribute to project teams to produce original works or solve problems

3. **Research and Information Fluency**

   Students apply digital tools to gather, evaluate, and use information. Students:

   a. plan strategies to guide inquiry

   b. locate, organize, analyze, evaluate, synthesize, and ethically use information from a variety of sources and media

   c. evaluate and select information sources and digital tools based on the appropriateness to specific tasks

   d. process data and report results

4. **Critical Thinking, Problem Solving, and Decision Making**

   Students use critical-thinking skills to plan and conduct research, manage projects, solve problems, and make informed decisions using appropriate digital tools and resources. Students:

   a. identify and define authentic problems and significant questions for investigation

   b. plan and manage activities to develop a solution or complete a project

    c. collect and analyze data to identify solutions and make informed decisions

    d. use multiple processes and diverse perspectives to explore alternative solutions

5. Digital Citizenship

Students understand human, cultural, and societal issues related to technology and practice legal and ethical behavior. Students:

    a. advocate and practice the safe, legal, and responsible use of information and technology

    b. exhibit a positive attitude toward using technology that supports collaboration, learning, and productivity

    c. demonstrate personal responsibility for lifelong learning

    d. exhibit leadership for digital citizenship

6. Technology Operations and Concepts

Students demonstrate a sound understanding of technology concepts, systems, and operations. Students:

    a. understand and use technology systems

    b. select and use applications effectively and productively

    d. troubleshoot systems and applications

    c. transfer current knowledge to the learning of new technologies

National Educational Technology Standards for Teachers (NETS•T)

All classroom teachers should be prepared to meet the following standards and performance indicators.

I. Technology Operations and Concepts

Teachers demonstrate a sound understanding of technology operations and concepts. Teachers:

   A. demonstrate introductory knowledge, skills, and understanding of concepts related to technology (as described in the ISTE National Educational Technology Standards for Students).

   B. demonstrate continual growth in technology knowledge and skills to stay abreast of current and emerging technologies.

II. Planning and Designing Learning Environments and Experiences

Teachers plan and design effective learning environments and experiences supported by technology. Teachers:

   A. design developmentally appropriate learning opportunities that apply technology-enhanced instructional strategies to support the diverse needs of learners.

   B. apply current research on teaching and learning with technology when planning learning environments and experiences.

   C. identify and locate technology resources and evaluate them for accuracy and suitability.

   D. plan for the management of technology resources within the context of learning activities.

   E. plan strategies to manage student learning in a technology-enhanced environment.

III. Teaching, Learning, and the Curriculum

Teachers implement curriculum plans that include methods and strategies for applying technology to maximize student learning. Teachers:

A. facilitate technology-enhanced experiences that address content standards and student technology standards.

B. use technology to support learner-centered strategies that address the diverse needs of students.

C. apply technology to develop students' higher-order skills and creativity.

D. manage student learning activities in a technology-enhanced environment.

IV. Assessment and Evaluation

Teachers apply technology to facilitate a variety of effective assessment and evaluation strategies. Teachers:

A. apply technology in assessing student learning of subject matter using a variety of assessment techniques.

B. use technology resources to collect and analyze data, interpret results, and communicate findings to improve instructional practice and maximize student learning.

C. apply multiple methods of evaluation to determine students' appropriate use of technology resources for learning, communication, and productivity.

V. Productivity and Professional Practice

Teachers use technology to enhance their productivity and professional practice. Teachers:

A. use technology resources to engage in ongoing professional development and lifelong learning.

B. continually evaluate and reflect on professional practice to make informed decisions regarding the use of technology in support of student learning.

C. apply technology to increase productivity.

D. use technology to communicate and collaborate with peers, parents, and the larger community in order to nurture student learning.

VI. Social, Ethical, Legal, and Human Issues

Teachers understand the social, ethical, legal, and human issues surrounding the use of technology in PK–12 schools and apply that understanding in practice. Teachers:

A. model and teach legal and ethical practice related to technology use.

B. apply technology resources to enable and empower learners with diverse backgrounds, characteristics, and abilities.

C. identify and use technology resources that affirm diversity.

D. promote safe and healthy use of technology resources.

E. facilitate equitable access to technology resources for all students.

Index